USBORNE
LAW
FOR BEGINNERS

Written by
Rose Hall and
Lara Bryan

Illustrated by
Miguel Bustos
and Anna Wray

Law experts:
Natasha Jackson and Will Martin

Designed by Freya Harrison

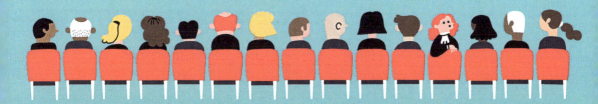

Contents

What is law?	4
Why do we need laws?	6
How does the law work?	8
Right and wrong	10
It isn't black and white	12

Chapter 1: Criminal law — 15
An unlucky accident, or a serious crime? Follow a story to see what happens, and who gets involved, from a person's arrest to trial and beyond.

Chapter 2: Civil law — 31
Most law isn't about crime and punishment – it's about settling arguments, and making sure people behave fairly to each other. This is 'civil' law.

Chapter 3: How is law made? — 43
Laws used to be made by leaders with limitless powers. Today, most laws are made by elected politicians, who have to follow all sorts of rules.

Chapter 4: Law across borders — 61
Are there laws that the *whole world* has to obey? How are those made – and how are they enforced?

Chapter 5: Human rights 77
Some of the most important laws, or *rights*, are meant to ensure that all people can live safe, healthy lives with equal opportunities. But does this actually happen?

Chapter 6: Justice 89
Justice means fairness. It's what law is all about, isn't it? But are laws *themselves* fair? And what about the system that enforces the law – is that fair?

Chapter 7: Big questions 103
Often in law, there are questions that don't have simple answers. Read some of the the arguments and see if you can make up your own mind.

Chapter 8: What next? 115
What about YOU? Could you be a lawyer, or a lawmaker, or a law enforcer?

Glossary 125
Index 126
Acknowledgments 128

Usborne Quicklinks

For links to websites where you can find out more about law of all kinds and across all countries, go to **usborne.com/Quicklinks** and type in the title of this book.

Please follow the internet safety guidelines at Usborne Quicklinks. Children should be supervised online.

What is law?

Law – or the law – is a set of rules about how a large group of people should behave, often covering a whole country. Laws are a little like the rules in a family or school, but more serious and official.

Yelling or running in the school halls might break a *rule*, but they don't break *the law*. Here are some things that are against the law in most places:

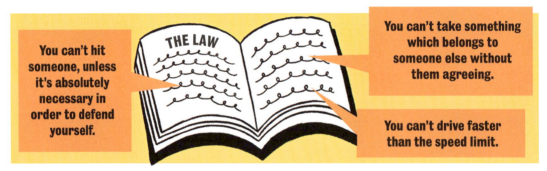

In some situations, the most powerful person in a group simply makes up the rules. But usually, rules are agreed upon through a careful process.

The process for deciding a *law* is more official. Laws are created by people who hold positions of power in the country, typically politicians.

To try to get people to follow rules and laws, anyone who breaks one is made to face the consequences. This is how it works at Deepdale School.

The consequences of breaking the *law* are worse than detention. People are given punishments, called **sentences**, such as:

Fines – sums of money you pay to the government

Time locked up in prison

Community service, which means working for free to help the community

Officials, such as the police or judges, have the power to hand out punishments when someone breaks a law.

How does the law work?

Law is all about solving problems – anything from a small argument to a murder – in the fairest way possible. Some of the ways people have found of making the process work date back thousands of years.

Going to court

Rather than settle arguments themselves, people can take a problem to **court**. A court is a group of people who come together to decide how to apply the law. It's also the name for the place they meet. The oldest known courts were in ancient Egypt, around 5,000 years ago.

Writing laws

It's harder for people to make up rules for their own benefit when laws are written down. The oldest written laws to be discovered are around 4,000 years old, from ancient Mesopotamia, now Iraq.

Talking to lawyers

It can be tricky to follow laws and courts. That's where **lawyers** come in – professionals trained to advise and represent people in court. The first lawyers worked in ancient Rome around 2,000 years ago.

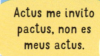

Finding proof

A court can't just *decide* that someone is guilty. It needs to see **evidence** that proves it – and it's up to the accusers to provide it. This idea is known as 'innocent until proven guilty' and dates back to ancient Roman law.

Judging fairly

The person who is in charge of a court and makes sure a case is dealt with according to the law is called a **judge**. To do their job properly, judges can't let money or powerful people influence their decisions.

In Britain, until the 18th century, kings and queens used to be able to fire judges they didn't agree with.

Justice

The point of all these processes – going to court, writing laws, finding proof – is to carry out **justice**.

This image shows Lady Justice. She's a symbol that's been used for centuries to explain what justice means.

Here's what she stands for:
- a blindfold shows that everyone should be treated the same by the law, whether they're rich or poor, powerful or weak.
- scales show that the evidence on both sides of the argument needs to be weighed up fairly.
- a sword shows that the law can punish and protect.

Right and wrong

Many people think the law is based on a deep sense of what's right and wrong – or in other words **moral** and **immoral**. But it's often not that straightforward. For example, all of these situations are, or used to be, illegal. But do you think they're all *immoral*?

Robbing someone

Wearing purple

Murder

Trading on a Sunday

Parking in the wrong place

Most people agree that certain things such as stealing and murder are *immoral* and should be illegal. But lots of illegal things aren't necessarily *immoral*. There are all sorts of other reasons why something might be against the law.

Some things are illegal just because someone has the POWER to say they are.

In 16th-century England, Queen Elizabeth I issued a law saying that only royals could wear purple.

NO MORE PURPLE FOR YOU!

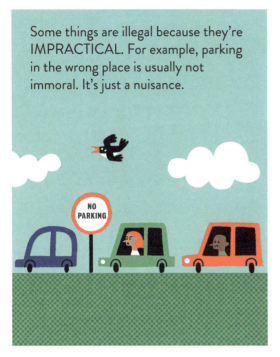

You may disagree with some of these examples. Laws aren't universal – what's illegal in one country might be seen as perfectly fine in another.

When a wrong becomes a right

People's idea of what is right and wrong changes over time, so laws do too.

It can take time to convince people in power to change laws or get new ones made. Find out more about how this happens in chapter 3.

11

It isn't black and white

It may sound simple to make certain acts, such as stealing, illegal. But people take things that don't belong to them in all sorts of situations. The law has to be clever enough to take this into account. Here's how.

Words matter

The wording of a law can seem like something a robot might say. That's because the words are carefully chosen to make it clear what's allowed and what's not. This can make laws hard to understand. For example, this is what the law on theft says in the United Kingdom:

> A person is guilty of theft if he or she dishonestly appropriates property belonging to another with the intention of permanently depriving the other of it.

Wondering what this all means? Don't worry, you aren't the only one!

"Dishonestly appropriates property" means taking something without the owner saying it is OK.

So you can't just take a skateboard from your friend's garage – that's theft.

I'm sure Pete won't mind....

But if you can prove that your friend gave you permission to take it, then that's not theft.

Can I borrow your skateboard tomorrow?

Yep sure! It's in the garage. Help yourself.

"The intention of permanently depriving" means having no plans to give the thing back.

This part of the law was important in a case in the 1960s, when a man took a painting from the National Gallery in London.

The man tried to use the painting as a bargaining tool to persuade the gallery to donate money to charity.

SEND £140,000 AND THE PAINTING WILL BE RETURNED.

It didn't work. Eventually, he gave the painting back and owned up to what he'd done.

Here you go.

When his case went to trial, he was found **not guilty** of theft of the painting because he had no intention of keeping it. But he did have to go to prison for three months for stealing the *frame*, as he hadn't given that back.

People decide

There is always a bit of wiggle room in the interpretation of a law, however precise its wording. That's because in the real world, laws are applied by human beings, who consider a person's situation when deciding how strict to be.

For example, what do you think should happen if someone stole food because they were desperately hungry?

In New York in 2019, police were called when a hungry woman stole food from a shop.

⬇

Instead of arresting her, they paid for her shopping.

In Italy in 2016, a homeless man took cheese and sausages from a shop.

⬇

A court ruled that he *couldn't* be guilty of theft because he was starving.

- Can the police arrest innocent people?
- Why do some judges wear wigs?
- What happens if a judge or jury make a mistake?
- What's a bail hearing?
- Why do people punish criminals anyway?

1. Criminal law

Many important laws are designed to protect people, or businesses, from harm. When someone breaks one of these laws, it is called a **crime**.

Starting from the moment a crime is suspected, all sorts of different people help get to the bottom of what happened. This includes **police officers**, **lawyers**, a **judge**, and a **jury**. Together, their job is to make sure that anyone guilty of a crime is punished.

In this chapter, you can follow the story of an imaginary crime. The story is set in Newcastle, England. In another country, the details of how the law works might be slightly different.

Something fishy

Police officers are usually the first officials to get involved after a crime has been committed. That may be because someone reports the crime to the police. Or the police might spot something suspicious themselves.

This is Tarak. He's feeling cheerful because he's recently won a lot of money in a lottery.

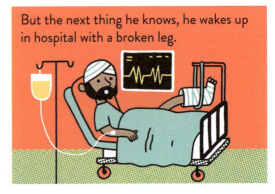

But the next thing he knows, he wakes up in hospital with a broken leg.

A police officer tells Tarak that a wheel fell off his car, making him swerve off the road and crash into a tree.

When the police inspect his car, they find that three of the four nuts connecting the wheel to the car were missing.

Hmmm... SUSPICIOUS.

Digging for clues

The police think that someone had tampered with Tarak's car, so they start an **investigation** – a search for more information. They gather **evidence**, which might prove that a crime was committed.

They look for fingerprints on Tarak's damaged car.

They watch footage from local surveillance cameras.

They interview Tarak, his girlfriend Elaine, and his co-workers.

Under arrest

The police suspect that Elaine tried to kill Tarak in order to get his lottery winnings, so they **arrest** her for the crime of attempted murder. They take her to a police station and ask her questions in a recorded interview.

To make sure that Elaine is treated fairly by the police, there are rules about how the police must behave. They must:

- have a good reason to arrest her
- tell her that anything she says could be used in court against her
- let her see a doctor if she needs one
- tell her that she is allowed to stay silent if she is asked a question
- let her get free advice from a lawyer
- let her make a phone call
- tell her why she is being arrested
- give her food and water regularly

Another limit is how long the police can hold someone in a police station without **charging** them (see the next page). Depending on the country and the crime, this is usually 24 or 48 hours, but can sometimes be even longer.

Making it official

If a police officer believes there is proof that someone committed a crime, the next step is to accuse them of it *formally*, which is known as **charging**. For the crime of attempted murder, the police must first persuade a government lawyer called a **prosecutor** that there is enough evidence.

> Elaine Mullins tried to kill her boyfriend by tampering with his car. I want to charge her with attempted murder.

> What evidence do you have?

> We found her fingerprints on the wheel that came off the car.

> How does she explain this?

> She says she touched the wheel to check the air pressure the other day.

> Could be a reasonable excuse. What else do you have on her?

← Prosecutor

> Uh. That's it.

> Sorry, that's not enough. We can only charge her if there is a realistic chance of a court finding her guilty. Otherwise it could just waste everyone's time.

> But my gut says she did it!

> Call back when you've found more evidence.

> You bet I will!

← Police officer

Prosecutors work on behalf of the government. In England and Wales, most work for the Crown Prosecution Service (CPS), while Scotland and Northern Ireland have separate systems. In the USA, prosecutors are known as **District Attorneys**.

What next?

The police officer finds more evidence against Elaine, so she *is* charged. Someone charged with a crime may go to court several times, so that important questions about the case can be answered. In court, the person is called the **defendant**, or the **accused**.

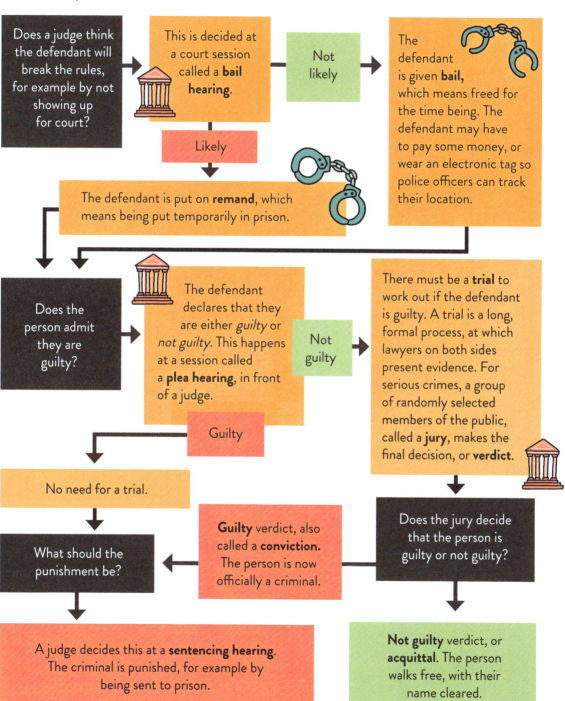

- Does a judge think the defendant will break the rules, for example by not showing up for court?
- This is decided at a court session called a **bail hearing**.
  - **Not likely** → The defendant is given **bail**, which means freed for the time being. The defendant may have to pay some money, or wear an electronic tag so police officers can track their location.
  - **Likely** → The defendant is put on **remand**, which means being put temporarily in prison.
- Does the person admit they are guilty?
- The defendant declares that they are either *guilty* or *not guilty*. This happens at a session called a **plea hearing**, in front of a judge.
  - **Not guilty** → There must be a **trial** to work out if the defendant is guilty. A trial is a long, formal process, at which lawyers on both sides present evidence. For serious crimes, a group of randomly selected members of the public, called a **jury**, makes the final decision, or **verdict**.
  - **Guilty** → No need for a trial.
- Does the jury decide that the person is guilty or not guilty?
  - **Guilty** verdict, also called a **conviction**. The person is now officially a criminal.
  - **Not guilty** verdict, or **acquittal**. The person walks free, with their name cleared.
- What should the punishment be?
- A judge decides this at a **sentencing hearing**. The criminal is punished, for example by being sent to prison.

Getting ready for the trial

Elaine pleads *not guilty* to attempted murder, so her case will go to a trial. In theory, Elaine could defend *herself* in court. But law is complicated, so hardly anyone ever does that. Elaine is better off if a **defence lawyer** acts on her behalf. Here are all the different people who get involved...

This is the **prosecution lawyer**, acting on behalf of the government. At the trial, she will argue that Elaine is *guilty*.

These are Elaine's **defence lawyers**, who will argue that Elaine is *not guilty*.

In England, a lawyer who prepares a case before trial is called a **solicitor**...

...and a lawyer who stands up in court is called a **barrister**.

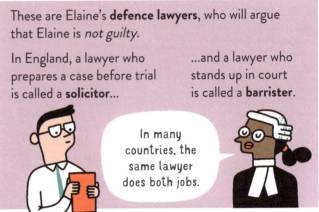

In many countries, the same lawyer does both jobs.

Ahead of the trial, both sides gather **evidence**. They also find people who have information that is relevant to the case. They are called **witnesses**.

These people will be witnesses for the prosecution.

Tarak   A vehicle expert

Elaine will be a witness for the defence. The person accused often acts as a witness, but not always.

I want to show the jury what a good person I am.

This is the **judge**. During the trial, the defence and prosecution will compete to present the most convincing case. The role of the judge is to make sure both sides play by the rules, a bit like a referee in a sports match.

One thing I do is to decide whether a piece of evidence can be used in court.

In some parts of Europe and South America, a special judge called an **investigating judge** finds evidence and questions witnesses ahead of the trial.

20

Did she do it?

Now it's the **trial**, where the prosecution tries to demonstrate that Elaine is guilty. Both sides present their evidence and witnesses, to try to convince the jury that their side of the story is true. The jury listens carefully. They must decide whether the prosecution has *proved* Elaine's guilt.

This is what a criminal trial for a serious crime looks like in England and Wales. Elsewhere, people might sit in different positions, but the principles are the same.

Generally, criminal trials are open to the public. This openness helps ensure a fair trial.

Public gallery

Journalist

Tarak

Witness box

Towards the end of the trial, both lawyers make a speech to the jury called a **closing argument**.

Prosecution lawyer

> Ladies and gentlemen of the jury, this was a heartless crime, motivated by Elaine's greed.

> Elaine persuaded Tarak to move his lottery winnings into their joint account before the accident. She did this to get his money if he died.

Elaine's family

> The night before the accident, *someone* removed three of the four wheel nuts on Tarak's wheel. With only one nut left, the wheel fell off. The vehicle expert said that Tarak is lucky to be alive.

> You can be sure that Elaine is guilty. Her fingerprints were on the car wheel and on the missing wheel nuts. A sandwich found in the same bag as the wheel nuts contained traces of Elaine's saliva, proved by a scientific test.

> Did she aim to kill Tarak? Yes. Just before the accident, she did an internet search for, "How to cause a fatal car accident", then read many articles. One specifically suggested removing wheel nuts.

A judge is in charge of the trial and makes sure it is run fairly. At the end, she sums up the facts of the case and explains the law to the jury to help them make their decision.

Wigs

In the UK and some African countries, lawyers and judges wear wigs when they are in court. This dates back to the 17th century, when it was fashionable for lots of rich people to wear wigs. Fashion changed, but judges and lawyers kept on wearing them. Some argue that wigs give courts a solemn and formal air.

Either Tarak or Elaine must be lying...

The clerk records decisions.

The jury is made up of twelve members of the public aged from 18-75.

Defence lawyer

Ladies and gentlemen of the jury, this was a horrific crime, but it was not committed by Elaine.

Tarak moved his lottery money into the joint account because the couple was planning a holiday. Text messages between them show this.

Elaine's fingerprints were on the wheel of the car because she had checked the air pressure.

Elaine did put that sandwich in the bin, but it is a coincidence that wheel nuts were found in the same bag.

As for the article, my client clicks on silly things online when she is tired. It means nothing. That night, she also clicked on a video of a cat singing.

For these reasons, you cannot be sure that Elaine is guilty. Security camera footage shows several other people entering the car park. One of *them* is the criminal, not Elaine.

Elaine sits in an area at the back called the **dock**.

← Defendant

Dock

Guilty act? Guilty mind?

For someone to be *guilty* of a crime, the law says that two things must be proven: that the person committed the harmful physical act, and that they knew what they were doing when they did it. These are known as *actus reus*, which is Latin for 'guilty act' and *mens rea*, meaning 'guilty mind'.

The jurors in Elaine's trial now discuss their decision, or **verdict**. They unpick the problem by talking through the different parts of the crime.

The act

The jurors remember some things the judge told them during the trial.

It is up to the prosecution to convince the jury that the defendant is guilty.

The defence does *not* have to convince the jury that the defendant is *innocent*, just that the prosecution's arguments are not good enough.

If the jury is not *sure* whether the defendant is guilty, they **must** give a verdict of *not guilty*.

These points are important, because anyone accused of a crime is assumed to be **innocent until proven guilty**.

The mind

Did Elaine intend to kill Tarak?

I think she was trying to kill him. Because of the lottery money.

Maybe she wanted to scare Tarak, but didn't actually want to kill him?

But they were planning a holiday. Why plan a holiday if she was going to kill him?

Even if she didn't intend to kill him, she *must* have known there was a high chance he would die.

Any reasonable person would know that a wheel falling off would be extremely dangerous!

She specifically searched the internet for "*deadly* car crash".

I don't think that reading one blog is enough to prove that she wanted to kill him.

What if she thought about killing him at that moment but didn't actually want to kill him?

But it was 11 different blogs. She can't have just idly clicked on 11 different car crash blogs.

If she changed her mind later, she should have warned him not to drive the car.

The jurors talk among themselves for hours, until they all support the same decision, called a **unanimous verdict**. What would you do if you were on this jury?

25

Why sentence?

The jury in Elaine's trial decides that she is guilty of attempted murder. It's up to the judge to decide how she will be sentenced. But what is the point of sentencing criminals? This Venn diagram shows that there are different types of sentences, and different reasons to sentence people.

To punish criminals

Making someone do something they don't want to do is punishment for the hurt they inflicted. All the sentences inside the purple area shown on the opposite page have an element of punishment in them.

To put people off

Some sentences are scary or unpleasant so they discourage people from committing crime. **Fines** and **prison** are examples. The most extreme is a **death sentence** – being killed as a punishment, which still happens in China, Saudi Arabia and some parts of the USA. (Lots of people disagree with death sentences.)

To keep everyone safe

Some sentences are designed to stop dangerous people from causing further harm. This is one reason for locking someone up in prison. Someone who is less dangerous might be given a **community sentence**. This means they are free, but have to fulfil conditions, such as meeting often with a **Probation Officer**, who checks up on them.

To help criminals change their ways

If criminals learn new skills and get help when they need it, they may be less likely to commit crime again. This is called **rehabilitation**. For example, a criminal may be sent on an anger management course, either in prison or as part of a community sentence. Or they may be given a chance to gain skills through unpaid work.

To make up for what they did

Some sentences are designed to enable a criminal to try to repair the damage they caused. For example, a community sentence might include unpaid work that benefits the local area, such as scrubbing off graffiti. Or, a criminal might have to pay money to the victim, which is called **compensation**.

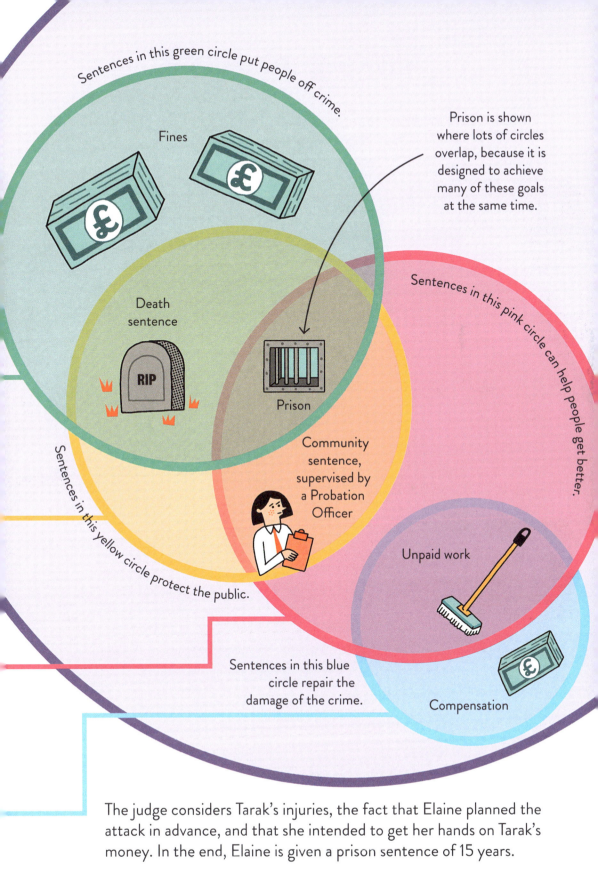

The judge considers Tarak's injuries, the fact that Elaine planned the attack in advance, and that she intended to get her hands on Tarak's money. In the end, Elaine is given a prison sentence of 15 years.

Making an appeal

Many people, when found guilty, want to **appeal** against the verdict. This means asking another court to look at their case. But a case only goes to appeal if it seems that something went wrong at the original trial. Here are some examples...

Mishandling of evidence

In Elaine's case, I stored the sandwich in the same container as her saliva sample. So her saliva might have contaminated the sandwich accidently.

Jury mistakes

Jurors are not allowed to talk to anyone except each other while we are making up our minds. But I contacted Elaine on Instagram to ask if she did it...

Errors by the judge

Maybe I made a mistake when I summed up the facts of the case, or when I explained the relevant laws to the jury?

Failings by defence lawyer

I didn't bother to get in touch with a witness who could have made Elaine's case much stronger.

A special court called an **appeal court** makes a decision about whether errors were made. Crucially, it also decides whether these errors made a difference to the outcome of the trial. An appeal court will say one of these things:

- No mistakes were made. The verdict still stands.
- Mistakes were made, but the verdict still stands.
- Big mistakes were made, and the verdict should be changed.
- Big mistakes were made, and a new trial is needed, known as a **retrial**.

Appealing against an appeal

It is even possible to appeal against the decision of an appeal court. Courts have different names in different places. But everywhere has a series of courts, which are ranked in importance.

Least important:
Trial courts

Middle importance:
Appeal courts

Most important:
Highest court of appeal

A country has lots of trial courts. There is only one judge in each courtroom.

Some places have different trial courts for minor offences and serious crimes. Juries only play a role in trials for serious crimes.

Appeal courts review whether trial courts made mistakes. They consider the details of the specific case in front of them.

Trial courts have to follow what they say.

The highest court of appeal doesn't look at questions of *fact*, but questions of *law*.

Every case is overseen by a group of judges. They decide how the law should be applied, not just in the specific case in front of them, but also in similar cases occurring in the future.

Each country only has one of these courts. Trial courts and appeal courts must follow what the highest court says.

Here's an example of a case that went all the way to the highest court.

In 2008, in Louisiana, USA, a man named Robert McCoy was charged with murder. He wanted to plead "not guilty", but during the trial, his own lawyer said that he was guilty.

At McCoy's trial...

...the jury found him guilty of murder.

When McCoy appealed...

...the appeal court ruled against him. They said that although his lawyer went against his wishes, this didn't change the outcome of the trial because there was so much evidence against him.

The highest court...

...ruled in favour of McCoy. It said that a defendant must always be able to choose to plead "not guilty". The court decided this was such a big error that McCoy should have a retrial.

29

- Do I HAVE to go to school?
- Is it against the law to copy someone?
- How do footballers' contracts work?
- Can I marry anyone?

2. Civil law

Grown-ups argue about all kinds of things, from money, to relationships, to a faulty item from a shop. Sometimes, just talking can solve the problem. But other times, you need legal experts to help people settle their differences.

This is what **civil law** is all about. It's the law that focuses on the relationships between people, companies and organizations – especially when things go wrong.

You hurt me!

In criminal law, if someone hurts you, the *government* takes the accused to court on behalf of the whole of society. In civil law, if someone hurts you, *you* take *them* to court and the outcome is very different...

Criminal

The guilty party is punished.

"You've been found guilty of deliberately breaking his leg. I'm sentencing you to 16 months in prison."

Civil

The victim is given money to make up for being hurt. This is known as **compensation**.

"You must pay him £1,000 to compensate for his twisted ankle."

In civil cases, an injury is known as a **tort**, which comes from the French word for 'wrong'. If a tort is serious enough, it might end up in a civil *and* criminal trial. As well as injuries, torts include...

...emotional harm

...damage to your property

As well as compensation, courts can also ask for some kind of action to make up for the harm caused, such as removing a damaging article.

...damage to your reputation, known as **defamation**

...deceiving someone for financial gain, known as **fraud**.

Whose fault?

What do you make of this tort case? In a Scottish café in 1928, May Donoghue became very ill after drinking a ginger beer with bits of dead snail in it. She ended up off work for a month. Whose fault do you think it was?

May's story was a turning point in British law. The high court's decision established that if anyone causes harm by *accident* by being careless, it's still their *fault*. This is known as **negligence**, and is the most common type of tort. So the factory owner paid May £200 in compensation.

Contracts

When two or more people make formal promises to each other, in writing or even in conversation, it's known as a **contract**. If either side doesn't carry out its promise, the law becomes involved. Here's how it works when a football club hires a footballer.

The footballer and the club discuss a list of things they will and won't do. All the details are written down in a contract, and they sign it to show that they've reached an agreement.

- The club promises to pay you £50 million per year…
- …to pay you a £15,000 bonus per match if we win
- …and to buy you a car and pay your rent.

- I promise to play for the team for at least two years…
- …to turn up to training, play each match and keep fit
- …and to not go to space*.

If you're tricked or pressured into agreeing to a contract, it isn't valid.

A contract is helpful because it gives certainty to both sides.

- He can't just leave whenever he wants to play for a better club.
- I know I'll be paid a salary even if I don't score in the next match.

If one side doesn't keep their promise, it's called a **breach of contract**, and they have to make up for it by paying compensation.

The amount of compensation can be agreed in advance. So footballers often negotiate a 'buy-out clause', which states how much compensation is due if they leave their club early.

Sometimes both parties can't agree on the right amount of compensation, and a court has to decide.

*As long as it's legal, anything goes. In 1999, Sunderland football club asked the footballer Stefan Schwarz to promise not to go to space and he agreed.

Buying things

Not all contracts involve sitting down and signing a piece of paper. In the eyes of the law, every time you buy something, it's as if the seller had signed a piece of paper saying, 'This thing is fit for purpose, as described and satisfactory.'

The newsagent would be in breach of contract if she sold a newspaper with some pages missing, for example.

Similarly, if you buy a car, you would expect it to be as the seller described it. But in 2015, the German carmaker Volkswagen was accused of making millions of cars that cheated pollution tests.

The cars were programmed to produce low levels of pollution when they were being tested. But on normal roads they produced around 40 times more pollution than was legal.

That's not what I paid for!

In the USA, people can take a company to court as a group – a type of case called **group litigation**. So that's what hundreds of thousands of Volkswagen's customers did.

We want our money back!

In October 2016, a US court ordered Volkswagen to pay around $10 billion in compensation to these customers.

What about me?! Birds don't get compensated for the all the extra pollution to our lungs.

Family law

Some common situations might *look* like private issues that shouldn't concern a lawyer or a judge. But in every country there are rules about each of these situations. This is known as **family law**.

Getting married

In most countries, you can get a relationship officially recognized by getting married or registering a civil partnership or union. It's a legal act that gives you rights and responsibilities, such as making medical decisions for the other person if they are too ill to do so.

Breaking up

To end a marriage or a civil partnership, you have to prove to the courts that the relationship is over and can't be saved. Only a court can make it official.

Often, couples that break up have to make big decisions. If they *can't* agree, then they might go to court.

How do we split our money?

Who gets to live in our home?

Where will I live?

When will I see my kid?

Adopting a child

Becoming the parent of someone else's child is known as **adoption**. It has to be approved by the courts.

These are our adoptive parents.

Raising children

There are even laws to make sure parents do their job properly, such as making their kids go to school. If they can't look after them, local government can take parents to court.

Mmm, if I don't go to school, my Dad might get into trouble.

Family rights

A lot of the rights we take for granted to do with love and family haven't been around for long, and still aren't recognized in some countries.

Interfaith marriage

This is the right to marry someone of a different religion. In India, interfaith marriage became legal for everyone in 1954.

I'm Hindu.

I'm Muslim and we can finally get married.

Same-sex marriage

This is the right for two men or two women to get married.

In 2010, the Netherlands became the first country in the modern world to allow same-sex marriage.

Now it's legal in around 30 countries.

Property rights

The rights to own, buy, sell and inherit property are known as **property rights**. Until the 20th century, in many places women did not have the same property rights as men, and some still don't.

Protest, Tunisia 2019

Currently, in Tunisia when parents die, their money is split so that sons get twice as much as daughters.

Planning a family

The idea that people should be able to choose if and when to have children is known as **family planning**. In practice, this can mean using methods known as **contraception** to avoid getting pregnant.

Contraception used to be illegal in Ireland. I took the Irish government to court and got the law changed in 1973.

Mary McGee, campaigner

A change in the law doesn't always change people's behaviour. For example, in India, it can sometimes be hard for couples of different faiths or backgrounds to be accepted by their communities.

37

This land is mine

Ideas about property change over time. Sometimes people have to fight for those changes to get recognized by law.

In the 18th century, English sailors found a vast land that they'd never seen before.

"We've discovered a NEW land! Let's call it Australia! We can live here and farm here – anything we want!"

"Hang on, our people have been living here for over 65,000 years!"

"Well now it's OURS."

Over the next century, more and more Europeans moved to Australia, claiming the land as theirs. This is a process known as **colonization**.

"It's perfectly legal! Nobody *owned* this land until we got here."

Until the 1990s, Australian land law was based on an idea that until the Europeans arrived, the land belonged to *nobody*. This idea is known as *terra nullius*.

This meant that Indigenous Australians – people whose families had been living in Australia long before the Europeans – didn't have legal land rights.

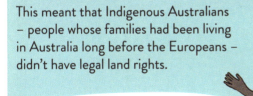

"In 1977 when my dad died, I wasn't allowed to inherit his land. The government said it had never belonged to us. So I took the case to court."

Eddie Mabo, Indigenous land rights activist

After 10 years of court cases, the Supreme Court ruled that Australia was NOT *terra nullius*, and recognized Indigenous Australians' right to the land.

(But they still haven't got it all back...)

It's MY idea

As well as owning things you can touch, such as land, you can also own ideas or information. This is known as **intellectual property** and there are special laws to protect it.

Copyright

The law of **copyright** stops anyone from using someone's work without their permission – whether it's art, writing, music, film, TV or online content.

Patents

When you invent something, you can register a **patent** for it. This stops anyone else from making or selling your invention for a number of years.

I've patented this idea for an umbrella hat so that nobody can copy it.

Artists and inventors often depend on these laws to make money from their work. But with some inventions, such as life-saving drugs, that might seem unfair.

THE DAILY NEWS
South Africa, April 2001

EXPENSIVE DRUGS COST LIVES

In South Africa, hundreds of thousands of people die every year from a disease known as AIDS because they can't afford treatment.

WHY DO THE DRUGS COST SO MUCH?

Drug companies spend *millions* on inventing a drug. By patenting it, they can sell the drug to customers and make that money back. But what's a fair price?

Charging poor people sky-high prices for drugs is wrong. We'll have to buy cheaper drugs from other countries.

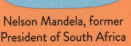

Nelson Mandela, former President of South Africa

COURT BATTLE OVER CHEAPER DRUGS

A group of drug companies took the South African government to court, to stop it getting cheaper drugs from suppliers abroad.

After protests around the world, the drug companies dropped the case. They also lowered the price of the drugs from $10,000 per year per person to $1,000.

You don't *have* to go to court

Going to court can be expensive and time-consuming. Another option is to get the help of a person known as a **mediator**. He or she won't take sides and will try to find a solution that works for everyone – whether it's a dispute between businesses, families or even kids in the playground.

- What's the 14th amendment?
- Are all laws written down?
- How do you stop a leader from becoming too powerful?
- Why is the US Constitution so important?
- Can you take a president to court?

3. How is law made?

Some people have the power to make new laws. This is often politicians who sit in a **parliament**, but it can also be judges, kings and queens, or even religious scholars. It happens in different ways in different countries.

Basically, everywhere has its own rules about who has power, and how new rules are made. Rules about rule-making are known as **constitutional law**. Some countries, but not all, have their constitutional law written down in one handy document, called a **constitution**.

Sources of law

Law doesn't work the same way in every part of the world. Different countries have different **legal systems**. One difference is where the laws come from. Here are the most common sources.

Legislature

Most countries have a major part of government which has the job of making new laws. It's officially called a **legislature** or **legislative branch**, but it's often known as a **parliament**, **congress** or **assembly**.

Hundreds of politicians meet inside to debate and decide on laws.

Do you support the new law about scooters?

Not yet, it needs to change.

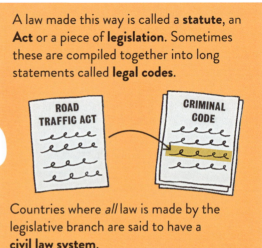

A law made this way is called a **statute**, an **Act** or a piece of **legislation**. Sometimes these are compiled together into long statements called **legal codes**.

Countries where *all* law is made by the legislative branch are said to have a **civil law system**.

Judges' decisions

Some places have a system called **common law**, which means that laws are established by judges' decisions in earlier cases.

1971, USA Supreme Court

We rule that the company broke the law, by refusing to hire Ida Phillips just because she is a woman with young children.

1974, USA

My current case is similar to Ida Phillips' case in 1971. Let me check what the judges decided then.

In any current case, a judge *must* follow the decisions taken by a higher court in previous, similar cases.

Religious texts

Some Muslim countries use a system of **Islamic law**. This comes from Islam's central religious text, the **Quran**, as well as another collection of important writings, the **Sunnah**. Experts in Islam – scholars – study these texts in detail.

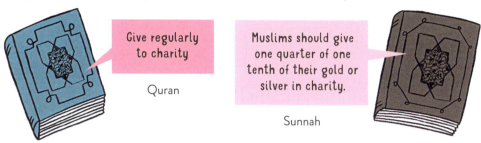

Give regularly to charity

Quran

Muslims should give one quarter of one tenth of their gold or silver in charity.

Sunnah

Scholars make laws about how the texts apply to modern life. For example, they've described exactly who should give to charity, and how often.

Customs

In some places, traditions that a community has followed for many years are considered to be laws, even though they aren't written down. This is called **customary law**.

In Inuit communities, a conflict between two people is resolved not in a court, but with a song duel.

Each person composes and performs a song which mocks the other in a clever, funny way. Whoever best entertains the rest of the community wins the dispute.

He is such a clumsy hunter... he can't even catch his own boots!

A mix...

The legal systems of many countries get their laws from a mixture of these sources. Turn the page to find out more...

What happens, where?

Here are some examples of different legal systems used around the world.

Canada uses common law alongside laws passed by its Parliament.

In **England and Wales**, **Northern Ireland**, **Scotland** and **Ireland**, some laws are made by parliaments or assemblies, and some is common law.

The **USA** uses common law as well as laws passed by its Congress.

My country used to be ruled by France, so our system looks like France's.

French-speaking African countries, such as **Senegal**, tend to have civil law systems.

Nigeria uses a mixture of common law, Islamic law and laws made by its National Assembly.

Chile, **Peru**, **Argentina**, and most other countries, in South America have civil law systems.

South Africa uses a combination of common law, customary law and laws made by its Parliament.

46

Hold on... what does 'civil law' mean again?

'Civil law' (as opposed to criminal law) can refer to laws about relationships between people. But beware! A 'civil law *system*' is something quite different. That means one with all laws written down in codes or legislation. And get this... both civil law systems *and* common law systems have *both* civil laws *and* criminal laws. Confusing, huh?

Most European countries have civil law systems, such as Spain and Lithuania.

Our legal system looks a bit like the ones in Germany and France, because we chose to copy them.

China

South Korea
Japan

Saudi Arabia uses Islamic law.

Saudi Arabia
Oman
Yemen

India

China, **South Korea** and **Japan** all use systems of civil law.

Yemen and **Oman** both use a mix of Islamic law and laws passed by their parliaments.

India uses a mix of common law, religious law, customary law and law made by Parliament.

Australia has a legal system similar to the English one, because we used to be controlled by Britain.

Us too! It's the same for some African and Caribbean countries, India, Canada, Malaysia and several more.

Australia

Australia and **New Zealand** both use common law alongside laws passed by their parliaments.

New Zealand

47

Judge-made law

Common law develops over time. With each new similar case, decisions by judges make laws more and more precise. Here's an example, from over 100 years ago in England...

In 1884, an English crew was shipwrecked off the coast of Africa. After weeks adrift in a tiny boat, they were desperate with hunger and thirst.

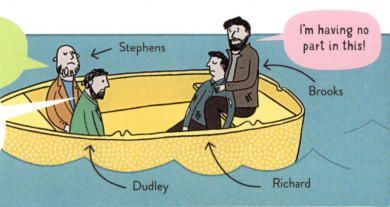

Back in England, Dudley and Stephens were charged with murder. Their defence lawyer argued that it was *necessary* to kill Richard Parker in order for them to stay alive. But after a trial and an appeal, the judges ruled that they *were* guilty of murder.

114 years later

Ever since the shipwreck case, "necessity" has not been accepted as a defence for killing someone in English law. But a situation happened in 2000 to test this law, when twins were born with their bodies attached.

If we don't separate the twins, both babies will die. If we separate them, Gracie should be fine, but Rosie will die.

We must separate the twins to save Gracie's life.

But we can't agree to an operation that will kill Rosie.

The doctors and parents disagreed, so the case went to court. The judges had to decide if the doctors should be allowed to end Rosie's life, because it was *necessary* to save Gracie's. In the end, they ruled that the twins *should* be separated. These were the reasons they gave:

This is different from the shipwreck case – the doctors gain nothing by taking Rosie's life.

This situation is not the kind of horrific, immoral act that the judges aimed to avoid back in 1884.

The doctors aren't *selecting* Rosie to die. She would die either way.

Following the operation, Rosie died, but Gracie survived and thrived.

NOW the law says that "necessity" is *not* a defence for killing someone. *Unless...*

...it is a very rare medical situation

...and to kill one person is very clearly the lesser of two evils

...and the victim isn't *selected* to be killed

Judge-made law is captured in a written report, called a **judgment**, published after a case. Each judge involved in the case describes his or her reasons for a decision. This tells other judges how to apply the law in future cases.

Laws made by Parliament

The politicians who sit in parliaments are generally chosen by members of the public, who want their politicians to make sensible laws. So while politicians debate the detail of a new law, they try to consider what the people who picked them might want. Here's how it works.

FRANCE, 2019

A new law begins as a draft, called a **bill**.

Bills are proposed by a politician who sits in Parliament.

People are going to LOVE my new bill. It will stop France throwing so much plastic away.

One of my proposals is that people will pay an extra charge – a **deposit** – every time they buy something in a plastic bottle. They'll get this back when they take the bottle back to the shop.

Next, politicians discuss the bill. In France, as in many countries, the Parliament is split into two decision-making parts – or **chambers** – the **Senate** and the **National Assembly**. Each bill goes to both, to ensure that a wide range of views are heard.

IN THE SENATE...

In general, I like this bill, but a scheme for returning plastic bottles is a silly idea! It will distract people from the real goal: to stop using plastic at all!

People who voted for me have been sending me angry letters about this bit of the bill.

Yes! Let's delete that bit!

I agree!

Senators

The politicians suggest edits to the text, called **amendments**, which are put to a vote. Then, the amended text goes to the other chamber for *more* debate.

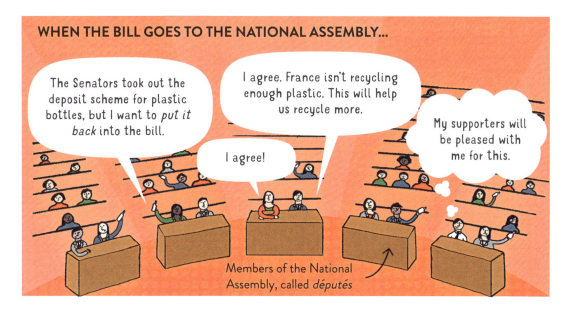

When there are disagreements between the two chambers, people try to find a compromise.

Once both chambers vote for exactly the same text, a bill can officially become a brand new law.

But for how long will it remain a law? After the next **election**, when a new group of politicians is voted into Parliament, they might withdraw existing laws and replace them with new ones – as long as enough *new politicians* agree to it.

Rules about making rules

Any organized group of people – whether it's a whole country or a local sports club – has rules about how the group is run, and how decisions should be made. These rules collected together are called a **constitution**.

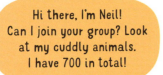

The US Constitution is the most famous example of a *country's* constitution. This is how it came about.

In the 1780s, 13 American States had recently fought a war to gain independence from England.

The states wanted to get along with each other, but without clear rules how to do this, there was tension between them.

So in 1787, a group of men got together to write a constitution for how they should be run as a single country: the United States of America.

Articles 1 and 2 set up a Congress with two parts – or chambers – and a President who must swear to defend the Constitution.

Article 3 says that the Supreme Court has the power to review whether laws go against the Constitution.

Article 5 says that to amend the Constitution, two thirds of both chambers of Congress must agree to it.

Some countries, such as the United Kingdom, don't have the laws about how to run the country collected and written down into one *single* constitution. But, even if it is written in different places, law of this kind is called **constitutional law**.

The US Constitution in action

Since 1787, the US Constitution has been amended 27 times. Some of the most ground-breaking amendments are about **slavery**, which is the horrific practice of owning another human being as if they were property.

From the 16th century to the 19th century, more than 10 million West African people were enslaved and taken to America.

Generations of people were held against their will, forced to work and traded for money.

When the US Constitution was written in 1787, it did not outlaw slavery. This was because many of the men who sat down to write the Constitution were slave owners themselves.

Slavery is morally wrong!

I refuse to give up my slaves. They are worth a lot of money to me.

The US Constitution officially declared that Black people were worth three fifths of what a White person was worth.

Then from 1861-65, there was a bloody war between the northern states, who opposed slavery, and the southern states, who supported it.

After the northern states won, the constitution was finally amended.

1865 Article 13 made slavery illegal, except as punishment for a crime.

1866 Article 14 made people formerly enslaved into citizens of the USA, and gave all citizens equal rights.

1869 Article 15 made it illegal to stop people from voting because of their race, or because they had previously been enslaved.

How Linda Brown changed history

One hundred years later, many laws still treated Black Americans differently, despite the Constitution giving them equal rights. One of these laws was struck down by the Supreme Court in 1954, thanks to a little girl called Linda Brown.

Eight year-old Linda had to walk a long way to school every day, even though there was a school much closer to her.

It's so far to walk and I am so cold.

That's because the local school was for White children. In Linda's state, Kansas, a law said that Black and White children should go to different, or **segregated**, schools.

Linda's dad tried to enrol her in the local school, but the principal refused. Prejudice against Black people – **racism** – was still deeply ingrained in many White people.

Black and White children mustn't mix! Otherwise, the next thing we know, Black and White children will marry. IMAGINE!

So Linda and her Dad took the case to court. It went all the way to the Supreme Court.

Segregated schools break the 14th Amendment, because Black and White children aren't treated equally.

Linda's lawyer

Lawyer for the Education Board

But the schools are of equal quality so it doesn't matter that they are separate!

A scientific experiment was used as evidence in Linda's case. In the study, Black children were asked whether they preferred a Black doll or a White doll.

This doll is black so it must be bad.

This doll is white so it must be good.

It showed that separating Black children made them feel inferior to White children.

The judges were moved by the doll study. They ruled that school segregation laws were *unconstitutional* so must be struck down.

Making Black children go to separate schools is damaging their confidence and holding them back. How can they have equal rights while this is the case?

It took time, but this case eventually led to schools becoming more integrated.

Is there a UK Constitution?

The UK is said to have an *uncodified* constitution, because its constitutional law isn't written down in one place. Instead, it's scattered around in a mixture of different documents, with some bits not even written down at all.

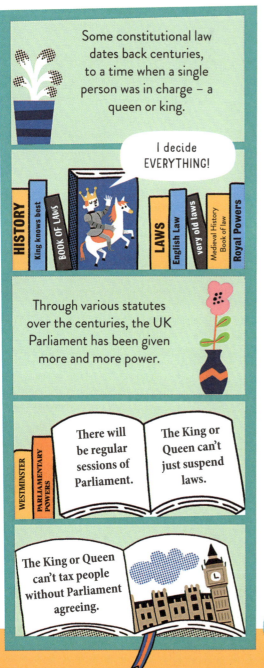

Some constitutional law dates back centuries, to a time when a single person was in charge – a queen or king.

I decide EVERYTHING!

Through various statutes over the centuries, the UK Parliament has been given more and more power.

There will be regular sessions of Parliament.

The King or Queen can't just suspend laws.

The King or Queen can't tax people without Parliament agreeing.

The current Queen still *technically* holds some historic power, known as the **Royal Prerogative**.

Every law made by Parliament must be approved by the Queen.

The Queen closes each session of Parliament (known as prorogation) and opens a new one.

The Queen has the power to send the army off to war.

But these days, there are some accepted, unwritten customs called **conventions** about who *actually* holds power.

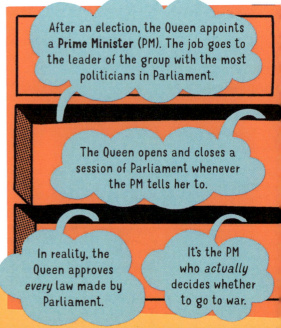

After an election, the Queen appoints a **Prime Minister** (PM). The job goes to the leader of the group with the most politicians in Parliament.

The Queen opens and closes a session of Parliament whenever the PM tells her to.

In reality, the Queen approves *every* law made by Parliament.

It's the PM who *actually* decides whether to go to war.

Some constitutional law is also captured in court judgments. Read on to find out about one example from 2019: a case in the UK's highest court, the Supreme Court.

Prime Minister vs Parliament

In 2019, the UK was on the brink of leaving the European Union (EU), a group of European countries which agree to trade with each other and make laws together.

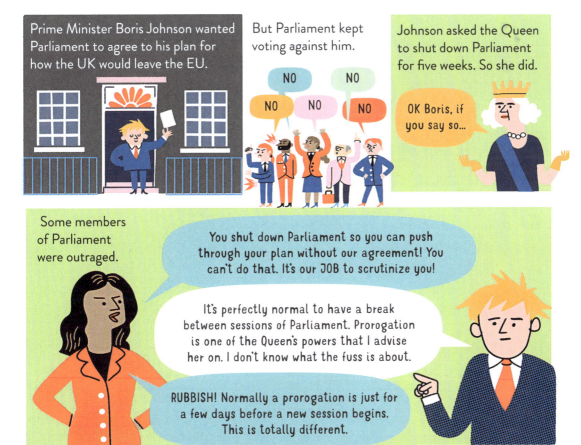

Prime Minister Boris Johnson wanted Parliament to agree to his plan for how the UK would leave the EU.

But Parliament kept voting against him.

NO NO NO NO NO

Johnson asked the Queen to shut down Parliament for five weeks. So she did.

OK Boris, if you say so...

Some members of Parliament were outraged.

You shut down Parliament so you can push through your plan without our agreement! You can't do that. It's our JOB to scrutinize you!

It's perfectly normal to have a break between sessions of Parliament. Prorogation is one of the Queen's powers that I advise her on. I don't know what the fuss is about.

RUBBISH! Normally a prorogation is just for a few days before a new session begins. This is totally different.

The Prime Minister was taken to court in both England and Scotland, and the case went to the Supreme Court. This is what the judges decided.

The Prime Minister *does* have the power to prorogue Parliament, but if it is shut for longer than usual, there must be a reasonable justification.

Johnson didn't explain why he shut Parliament for so long, so the prorogation was UNLAWFUL.

The arguments about leaving the EU rumbled on. But through this case, a piece of constitutional law was clarified: the Prime Minister can't just *choose* when to be scrutinized by Parliament.

Keeping power in check

The people in charge of a country have a LOT of power. But to stop any one person or group from seizing *too much* power, the constitutional law of many countries says that power must be split between three separate branches.

Executive branch

Normally, this is a single very important person, such as a **president, prime minister** or **chancellor**, or sometimes two people sharing power, such as a president and a prime minister. They run the country day-to-day with the help of a team, called a cabinet.

I'm Angela Merkel, Chancellor of Germany.

- The executive branch has the power to approve laws created by the legislative branch, see opposite.

- The executive branch has to *execute*, meaning carry out, the laws passed by the legislative branch...

  ...but can decide how quickly to do it, and which laws to prioritize.

- The executive branch appoints the senior judges that sit in the highest court, see opposite...

  ...but once appointed, the executive can't interfere in the judges' actual decisions.

This tree represents the three branches of power.

Legislative branch

This branch is called a parliament, congress or assembly.

The Bundestag is one part of Germany's Parliament.

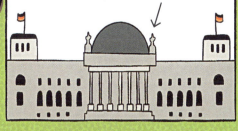

- The legislative branch can reject agreements, or treaties, that the executive branch has made with other countries.

- The legislative branch has committees on different subjects, which scrutinize what the executive branch is doing, and pressure it to keep its promises.

- The legislative branch creates laws, so it can tell the executive branch what to do.

Judicial branch

This is made up of senior judges, who make decisions in the highest court of the land.

We are three of Germany's most important judges.

- The judicial branch can rule that an action of the executive branch has broken the law. This principle, that no one is more powerful than the law, is called the **rule of law**.

- The judicial branch can decide that a law is 'unconstitutional', because it goes against rights that are laid out in the constitution.

Unchecked power

In 1933, Adolf Hitler was elected Chancellor of Germany. Although initially just in charge of the executive branch, he quickly grabbed power from the other two branches.

With nobody to hold him back, Hitler started a world war and ordered the murder of people he didn't like, including about six million Jewish people.

- Are there laws on the Moon?
- How does a new country get created?
- Can a country break the law?
- Can I go to any country I want to?
- Is one country *allowed* to go to war with another?

4. Law across borders

You can send a letter *anywhere* around the world. You've probably never thought about it, but it's only possible because every country has agreed on a common system for mail. There are all sorts of international agreements like this. They're part of a collection of rules and laws known as **international law**, which sets out how countries can work together to solve problems.

What is an international law?

Most international laws are called **treaties** – agreements made by governments to help their countries work together. They affect how people communicate, trade and move around the world. Here are a few examples.

I'm going to Mexico to learn Spanish this summer.

Countries sign agreements to allow planes to fly over and land in their country.

Air transport agreement

The weather forecast says it will rain tomorrow.

European countries have signed a treaty to create a joint weather forecasting agency.

European weather treaty 1975

When will the government commit to reducing the amount of pollution we produce?

THERE'S NO PLANET B!

Groups of countries can sign treaties promising to work together to solve big problems.

Paris Climate Agreement 2015
- We will pollute less
- We will stop temperatures rising by more than 2°C

Signed: _190 countries_

It's so tasty!

Some of the food you eat is probably grown or made in another country. Countries sign treaties promising to follow rules to make sure the food is safe to eat.

Food standards agreement

APPROVED

Signing a treaty is like signing a contract – countries then have to do the best they can to stick to the agreement. If a country breaks an agreement, it can be tried in an **international court**. Find out more on page 65.

62

"Hi Grandma! How's life in Sri Lanka?"

International laws aren't always written down. Some start out as **customs** – unwritten rules that countries have been following for a while.

You can make calls abroad because almost every country in the world has signed treaties on costs and communications equipment.

"My family just arrived in this country after fleeing a war back home."

Governments often make rules about who's allowed to move to their country. But they can't turn away **refugees** – people fleeing from a dangerous situation in another country. This has been an international custom for a really long time.

"Does everyone around the world have the right to go to school?"

Yes. International laws give the same human rights to everyone – BUT they're not always respected.

"If I robbed a bank and ran away to another country, would I get away with it?"

Individual countries can adopt international laws as part of their own laws.

Probably not! Countries sign agreements promising to work together to catch international criminals. Find out more on page 72.

A record of all treaties and other international laws is kept by the **United Nations**, an international organization of which almost every country in the world is a member.

63

How international law works

International law mostly developed after the Second World War. In 1945, to try to avoid *more* wars, leaders from around the world set up an international organization called the United Nations (UN). The UN sets rules for countries to follow and helps them settle arguments peacefully.

Common rules

Almost every country around the world is a member of the UN and agrees to follow its rules. Here are the most important ones.

- Respect human rights.
- Solve problems and arguments with other countries peacefully.
- Don't use force against other countries except in self-defence.
- Don't interfere in another country's affairs.
- Respect international law and keep promises made in treaties.

Countries can debate new rules every year at the **General Assembly**, in the UN headquarters in New York. Each country sends a person called a **delegate** to represent them.

Hello. Hallo. Hola! Witaj. Selamat datang.

If a country breaks any of the rules or threatens peace, the UN's **Security Council** can take action and impose **sanctions**. This can include making it illegal to trade goods with that country.

The Security Council is made up of 15 countries – five permanent members (China, France, Russia, UK and the US) and ten others that are elected every two years.

Settling disputes

The UN's **International Court of Justice** in the Netherlands exists to settle arguments between countries – but only if both countries agree to have their case heard by the court. Cases are heard by 15 judges elected from around the world.

You didn't tell us you were building polluting factories by the river on our shared border.

Lawyer representing Argentina

We did tell you! And we've used the greenest technology we can.

Lawyer representing Uruguay

ICJ judges

Uruguay should have told Argentina sooner, but we think the factories are safe enough to go ahead.

I disagree, but I've been outvoted by the others.

Argentinian judge

Punishing people

Sometimes countries can't or don't want to deal with very serious criminal cases. In these situations, the accused can be tried in the **International Criminal Court (ICC)**, whose judges are also elected from all around the world.

The ICC deals with **crimes against humanity**, such as mass murder, slavery and torture. It also hears cases of **war crimes**, such as using child soldiers, and **genocide** – the deliberate destruction of a group of people because of their nationality, religion or race.

2012

The ICC has found Thomas Lubanga, a rebel military commander, guilty of recruiting child soldiers in the Democratic Republic of Congo. He's been sentenced to 14 years in prison.

65

The law of countries

International law mostly focuses on the relations *between* countries. But what *is* a country in the eyes of the law?

Here's what makes Brazil a country:

1 It has a defined territory.

Olá!

2 It has people who live there all the time.

3 It has a government that manages and represents the country. The Brazilian government is based in the capital city called Brasilia.

Brasilia

Brazilian National Congress

A country has legal rights...

| To be a member of international organizations such as the UN. | To make its own decisions about its land and people. |

....and responsibilities.

| To respect international law. | To respect human rights and freedoms. | To settle disputes with other countries peacefully, without force or the threat of violence. |

Brazil is also a country because other countries recognize and treat it as one. Without this recognition, its rights and responsibilities might not be respected.

My country, Palestine, isn't recognized by around 50 countries. As a result it isn't a full member of the UN.

Making a new country

Sometimes, people in one place want to create a new country. Here are some of the international rules about how it can happen.

✘ Force

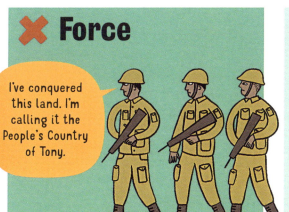

I've conquered this land. I'm calling it the People's Country of Tony.

Under international law, it's illegal to create a new country by using unlawful force. It's also illegal for other countries to recognize it as a country.

Vote

In 2008, after decades of war, people in the south of Sudan organized a vote. Most people said they wanted to form their own country, independent of the rest of Sudan.

The vote was recognized by every state around the world and South Sudan is now a member of the UN.

Independence from foreign rule

Under international law, people have a right to independence – to live in a country that isn't colonized by another country.

Between 1950 and 1970, around 60 countries that were colonized by European countries became independent again.

Malaysia, Cambodia, Algeria, Sudan, Vietnam

Even if you follow all the rules to form a new country, it's tricky to be truly independent if other countries – especially nearby ones – don't recognize your status.

Kosovo declared its independence from Serbia in 2008, after most Kosovans voted to leave. But Serbia still doesn't recognize us.

Can a *country* break the law?

In practice, countries can't break laws, only *people* can. But if a government, or anyone acting on its orders, does something illegal under international law, then the *country* is said to break the law. Here's an example.

In the 1970s, protests in the streets of Iran led to the overthrow of its unpopular leader, the Shah, who was backed and funded by the US.

In 1979, protestors surrounded the US embassy in Iran. They wanted the US to send the Shah back to Iran to face justice for crimes he was accused of.

The Shah fled to the US.

We won't let you out until the US sends back the Shah.

The protesters kept the US embassy staff hostage for over a year.

The US took a case against Iran to the International Court of Justice to try to get the embassy hostages released. The court had to answer these questions before coming to a decision.

Was a law broken?

A rule of international law is that embassies and their staff should never be attacked. So yes, a law has been broken.

Is a country responsible?

The government of Iran didn't ask the protesters to attack the embassy. But it didn't stop the protestors or free the hostages. So yes, the country is responsible.

The Court ordered the hostages to be released, which Iran ignored.

During and after the court case, the US and Iran used these other legal tools to try to end the hostage crisis.

Negotiation

Both sides met to talk through their demands and tried to make a deal.

We'll let the hostages go if you send back the Shah.

We'll think about it.

Retaliation

Under international law, countries are allowed to strike back to protect themselves. This is known as **retaliation**.

We've decided to confiscate any Iranian money that's in US bank accounts until the hostages are released.

US President Jimmy Carter

Mediation

This is when both sides ask a third party to help them find a solution. In this case, Algeria was asked to negotiate a deal. It got Iran to agree to return the hostages in exchange for the US returning the money.

The hostages are coming home!

Arbitration

Arbitration is a bit like going to court but both sides get to *choose* their judges. Since the hostage crisis, an arbitration tribunal has resolved around 4,000 disputes between Iran and the US.

You owe us! *No, we don't!*
You're the worst! *No, you're the worst!*
How much?! *You've got to be joking!*

Arguments between countries are often tricky to solve and can drag on for years. The legal system created for solving them isn't perfect. But it's still a whole lot better than using guns or bombs to deal with the problem.

69

Is war legal?

Using force, or threatening to use force, is usually illegal –
but there are some situations where it's considered ok.
In which of these situations do you think it might be legal to use force?

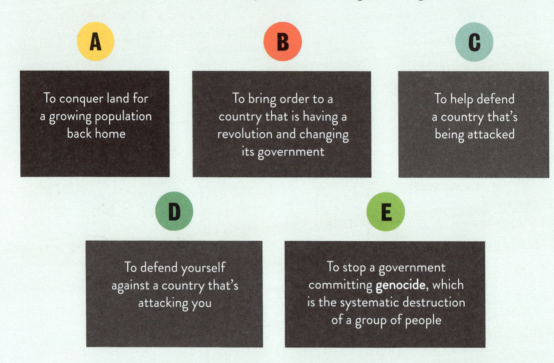

A To conquer land for a growing population back home

B To bring order to a country that is having a revolution and changing its government

C To help defend a country that's being attacked

D To defend yourself against a country that's attacking you

E To stop a government committing **genocide**, which is the systematic destruction of a group of people

Under international law it's legal to use force in self-defence (example D). It's also legal for the UN's Security Council to authorize the use of force against a country that is threatening world peace (example C) – but it rarely happens.

Some countries argue that it *should* be legal to use force to protect people's human rights in other countries (example E), but not everybody agrees. What do you think?

Using force, and interfering with what's going on inside a country is *illegal*!

But doing nothing is *immoral*! I think it's ok to use force to protect vulnerable people.

Countries must try doing everything else to help before using force, though!

The laws of war

If a war does break out – for whatever reason – there are special laws that apply to all countries in the world. These developed from a treaty first drafted in 1864, known as the Geneva Convention. Here are some of the most important rules.

Attacks should only be on military targets, such as airbases. This means it's illegal to target schools, hospitals or places of worship.

People who aren't involved in the fighting, known as **civilians**, must be protected.

Armies have a duty to look after their **prisoners of war** – people from the other side that are captured to stop them fighting.

International organizations that help victims, such as the International Committee of the Red Cross, must be allowed to do their job.

It's illegal to use certain weapons, such as poisonous gas, which hurt *everyone* – not just soldiers.

Armies should care for the wounded, even from the enemy side.

In wartime, causing unnecessary suffering, such as deliberately attacking civilians, is described as a **war crime**.

Under international law, countries whose armies have committed war crimes should make up for it, for example by giving money to rebuild a damaged city.

International criminals

A lot of serious crime, from selling drugs to terrorism, involves networks of criminals in different countries. Policing these crimes is a big job.

Interpol, the International Criminal Police Organization, helps police officers and justice officials across the world work together to fight international crime.

April 2020

We've just heard that the German government was tricked into giving money to a criminal gang. Here's what we know so far...

The German government wanted to buy millions of masks to protect its people from the disease Covid-19.

Wearing face masks helps stop the disease spreading.

They eventually found a supply from a Dutch company.

We'll sell you 1.5 million masks if you pay us €1.5 million up front.

Ok. We're paying now.

Just before the delivery...

We never received any money! Pay us a chunk now if you want the masks – €880,000 should do it.

That's odd. Ok, we'll send more money.

But the masks never turned up.

Where are they? And where's the money gone? We need to call the police!

We've worked out that the criminals copied the website of a real *Dutch company, and took all their orders and payments.*

Interpol, police forces and justice officials across Europe worked together to track down the money and arrest the criminals.

The criminals moved the money between different bank accounts to make it harder to track it down. But we managed to find it all!

**MISSING MILLIONS
Following the money trail**

The Irish police found €1.5 million of the stolen money in an Irish account and arrested a suspect.

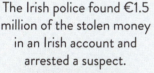

The Dutch police found €300,000 in a Dutch bank account and arrested two suspects.

A British bank found the rest of the money and stopped it from being moved to a Nigerian bank account.

Facing justice

Once someone has been caught, in which country should they be tried?

People usually have to be tried in the country where the crime was committed. When someone is sent to another country to face justice, it's known as **extradition**.

You can have him as long as you promise to treat him well and he gets a fair trial.

If someone is accused of committing a crime in *two* countries, it gets complicated. Should they be tried in each country?

Trying someone twice for the same crime seems unfair! Maybe both countries could work together on the case?

International law experts are still trying to work out the answer to this problem.

Space, air and sea

How much of the air and sea does a country own? This is the kind of question that the law of sea and space tries to answer. But whether it's high in the sky or deep in the sea, most people agree that we have to work together to protect it, and share what we know about it.

According to the Outer Space Treaty of 1967, space is free and nobody owns it.

Any discoveries and exploration of space should be for peaceful purposes and made for the benefit of everyone.

One giant leap for mankind.

Five partners – Europe, Russia, Japan, Canada and the US – own the ISS. Each partner is responsible for its own astronauts and equipment. This means five sets of laws apply on board.

The International Space Station (ISS)

Countries own the air above their territories, known as **airspace**. This was first set out in the Paris Convention on the Regulation of Aerial Navigation in 1919.

Pilots need to ask permission from a country before flying through its airspace.

Each country owns and has to look after things it sends into space.

This Chinese satellite sends information about the weather to forecasters all around the world.

The Law of the Sea Treaty sets out who owns different parts of the sea, and what you can and can't do in them.

Territorial sea

A country owns the waters up to 12 nautical miles (22km) from its coast (if it has one). Boats from other countries have to ask permission to sail here.

Exclusive economic zone

A country owns all the resources in the sea up to 200 nautical miles (370km) from its coast. But foreign boats and aircraft can move freely across the zone.

High seas

The rest of the sea is known as the High Seas. All countries have the right to navigate, fish, do research and lay cables and pipelines in the High Seas.

Find out about legal efforts to protect the environment on pages 112-113.

The ground at the bottom of the High Seas is owned by ALL countries. So any research and discoveries must be shared.

Does everyone have rights, even criminals?

What is discrimination?

Does freedom of expression mean you can say *anything*?

Who fights for human rights?

5. Human rights

There are some basic things that people need in order to live a decent life. They need physical things, such as food and shelter, as well as freedoms, such as the freedom to practise a religion if they want to. These are known as **human rights**.

Everyone *has* human rights, but not everyone gets to use them. That might be because they're living with poverty, violence or injustice. For the last few hundred years, lawmakers have tried very hard to write laws that explain what rights people have. This makes it easier to enforce those laws so these rights aren't ignored.

Your rights

Whatever the colour of your skin, your religion, abilities, wealth – EVERYONE has the same **human rights**. They're described in a document known as the **Universal Declaration of Human Rights**, created in 1948 by the United Nations. They include...

The right to education

The right to food, shelter and medical help

The right to think and say what you want

The right to move freely – to go from place to place without being stopped

The right to believe in what you want, and to change your mind

The right to choose your leaders

The right to a fair trial

The right to a safe, fairly-paid job

Until the age of 18, you have special **children's rights**, such as the right to play

It's often easy to take rights for granted, unless they're taken away from you.

How do human rights work?

Do we ALL have human rights? Isn't it just something people have in the richer parts of the world?

Animals have rights too, such as the right not to be treated cruelly.

You have rights from the moment you're born, simply because you're human. But although we all *have* them, not everyone's rights are respected.

Are human rights UNIVERSAL? Don't different places have different traditions?

Most countries have adopted laws that protect human rights. Human rights are based on values that are shared by cultures and religions all over the world.

What does being EQUAL in rights mean?

It means YOU have the same rights as everyone else. So it's not ok for someone to treat you differently, because of your gender, age or skin colour for example. This is known as **discrimination**.

Are some human rights more important than others?

No, they work as a whole. If you take away one right, it threatens all the others. For example if you don't have the right to work, then how can you get money to pay for food or shelter?

Can you take away people's rights, for example if they commit a crime?

No, but some rights can be *limited* to protect others – for example by sending someone to prison. Other rights, such as the right *not* to be treated cruelly, known as **torture**, *can't* be limited.

Rights in law

When rights are written into laws, it's easier to respect, protect and fulfil them. Here's how the right to **freedom of expression** is defined and guaranteed by New Zealand's Bill of Rights Act.

According to the Bill of Rights, everyone has the right to seek, receive and impart information and opinions of any kind in any form.

The law means the government has to RESPECT freedom of expression, and not interfere – even if it's being criticized.

The law PROTECTS freedom of speech – you can go to court if your right isn't respected.

The government also has to FULFIL this right, by helping people seek, share or receive information.

THE GOVERMENT HAS LET DOWN THE ELDERLY!

I got fired from a care home for criticizing the way residents were being treated. The judge ruled that I was sacked unlawfully.

I'm writing an article about the scandal in care homes. The government is helping by sharing recent care home inspection reports with me.

Freedom of expression is a key right that needs to be protected. Without it you can't point out other human rights problems, such as this one about people being mistreated in care homes.

So can I say *anything*?

Sometimes, expressing yourself can be harmful to other people or even a whole community. So in many countries lawmakers put some limits on freedom of speech in order to protect people.

It's illegal to say or post threatening or abusive things about someone based on their race, gender, sexuality or religion. This is known as **hate speech**.

Spreading lies about someone is illegal and is known as **defamation**.

@Wibble

Hey followers, big revelation today. @Sam101 is a THIEF.

To protect national security, there is some information that it's illegal to share.

The secret code to fire our nuclear weapons is...

BREAKING NEWS

But sometimes, powerful people might want to limit freedom of speech for their own ends – for example to avoid public criticism or cover up dodgy deals.

You can't say that!

Why?!

Because it makes me look bad.

Freedom of expression applies even to things you don't want to hear.

Well I've decided it's illegal and I'm sending you to prison.

Powerful person

Critic

YOU CAN'T LOCK HER UP!

Journalists and rights organizations work to uncover and call out human rights abuses. This puts pressure on governments and stops them getting away with things in secret, such as locking up their critics.

Making rights work

Even if the law protects your rights, in practice some people face more barriers to accessing their rights than others.

"I can't attend the meeting because it's in the middle of the working day."

PARENT TEACHER MEETING

Rescheduled
Thursday 8th October
at 2pm
3rd floor library

"That's Yom Kippur, I can't come that day either."

"There's no lift to the third floor so I'm going to struggle to get up there."

The school probably didn't *mean* to make it harder for these parents to get to the meeting. But what's happened here is **discrimination** – some people have been treated unfairly just because of an aspect of who they are, for example their disability. To protect people, many countries have anti-discrimination laws.

In 1999, in a divorce case, a Portugese court decided a child should live with the mother rather than the father.

"The court said it's because I'm in a relationship with a man. But I'm appealing against the decision at the European Court of Human Rights."

The European court found that the father had been discriminated against because of his sexuality.

The problem wasn't that the court had decided to send the child to live with the mother, but the *reason* for the decision.

It's now illegal in Portugal to take a parent's sexuality into account in divorce cases.

Multiple barriers

But what if you face discrimination for a *number* of reasons? That's the case for a lot of people, and the law often struggles to protect them.

I'm not Canadian, so this job advert is discriminating against me for two reasons.

JOB ADVERT
Canadian female nanny needed to look after kids aged 3 and 5.

Sometimes the reasons combine to create a whole new kind of discrimination.

We have a no-headscarf policy for employees in this shop, sorry.

I'm a non-muslim woman. That policy doesn't discriminate against me.

I'm a muslim man. That rule doesn't stop me working here.

So I'm being discriminated against specifically because I'm a *muslim woman*, not because I'm a muslim *or* because I'm a woman.

This kind of discrimination is known as **intersectional**, which is another word for overlapping. Lawyers and courts haven't yet agreed on a way of dealing with it.

Should there be special laws to protect people against *intersectional* discrimination?

Isn't it already against the law to discriminate against someone because of their gender or religion?

Yes, but in this case you can't *prove* either, because it doesn't discriminate against *all* muslims or *all* women. So without specific laws, it's hard to fight the case in court.

Fighting for rights

Many rights are now protected in law thanks to people known as **activists**, who campaign to bring about change. In the UK in the 1990s, activists campaigned for a new law to protect disabled people from discrimination in public spaces. Here's how they did it.

Protest

Gathering in groups to get people to listen to your concerns is known as **protesting**. Protesting is a human right.

WE DEMAND THE RIGHT TO TAKE THE BUS

ELEVATORS NOW!

I need to travel, shop and work just like everyone else. But it's really hard because those spaces aren't designed for people with a mobility disability like me.

Give us RIGHTS not charity.

Not all protests involve large groups of people. Small actions can make a difference too.

BUS STOP

We can't get on the bus because it doesn't have a ramp. But transport bosses won't install a ramp because they say there's no *proof* that disabled people want to take the bus.

So to give them proof, we're queueing for the bus even though we can't get on it.

It's the lack of action and discrimination that disables us, NOT our bodies.

Raising awareness

To get laws changed, you often need to change people's attitudes, by informing and educating them on the topic.

LIBERTY EQUALITY DISABILITY

I'm taking a university course in disability studies to learn about how to improve the situation.

Someone who works to understand the experience of people who face discrimination and takes action to support them is known as an **ally**.

Testing the law

Sometimes protestors take big personal risks and refuse to obey certain laws in order to make their point. This is known as **civil disobedience**.

Working together

Behind the scenes of most rights movements, there are many different organizations working to organize protests, gather signatures for petitions, pay lawyers to challenge laws, put pressure on politicians...

In 1995, after years of campaigning, the Disability Discrimination Act was passed. It requires people to make reasonable changes to workplaces and public spaces to make them welcoming to everyone. But change is slow and, whether it's building more ramps or changing attitudes, lots more progress is still needed.

Rights under threat

All over the world, there are still many cases of human rights not being respected. Spotting problems and speaking out is one way of trying to change that. Here are some problems to look out for.

Us vs Them

Journalists, politicians and decision-makers sometimes divide people into 'us' and 'them'. This makes *some* people's rights seem more important than others and helps justify discrimination. Here's an example from a British newspaper headline.

Us
children born to British parents

Them
increasing number of children born to non-British parents

50,000 KIDS LOSE FIRST CHOICE OF SCHOOL BECAUSE OF MIGRANT BABY BOOM

Some people think that migrant children are less deserving of school places. But the problem isn't the children; it's the lack of school places!

Picking and choosing

Governments might decide that some human rights are more important than others – especially in a crisis. For example, after a terrorist attack, the police might be given more power to arrest people and detain them for longer.

More arrests will help keep people safe!

But they're an attack on people's right to liberty.

Look, the threats are real – I think we have to prioritize people's safety.

Maybe. But will they remember to change the laws back when the situation gets better? It's usually easier to make laws tougher than it is to relax them...

Taking action

If you spot a problem, here are some ways of taking action.

- [ ] **Learn the facts**
  In order to bring about change, you need to understand the problem. Seek out facts from resources you can trust, such as news websites. And bear in mind that not everything you read or hear is true, it might just be one person's opinion – especially on social media sites.

- [ ] **Lend your support**
  Do some research to find out if there are charities or organizations already trying to deal with a problem. You could support them by raising money, sharing their message or volunteering your time.

- [ ] **Write to your representative**
  Get in touch with your local politician to share your views.

- [ ] **Challenge the media**
  Are their stories one-sided? Are they presenting *opinions* as facts?

  > Dear Editor,
  > I am writing to complain about...

- [ ] **Speak up**
  Defend and promote human rights in conversations with people around you.

  > Remember to be respectful and polite, you're more likely to be listened to.

It's not just the job of lawyers and judges and even politicians to fix the world – it's up to everyone to speak up against injustice, violence and discrimination, and make sure people's rights are respected.

6. Justice

People often talk about 'law' and 'justice' in the same breath. After all, the point of law, with all its rules, courts, lawyers and judges, is to deliver justice.
But what actually *is* justice?

And does anyone, whoever they are,
have the same access to it?

What is justice?

Justice means fairness. If justice has been done, then you tend to have a feeling that the morally right thing has happened. But this can mean a few different things.

For example, what does justice look like for this girl, Melia? Melia and her mother, Imelda, live near a big factory that makes chemicals. It emits lots of polluting gas.

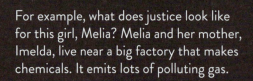
Melia has developed a serious illness because of the pollution.

My lungs feel tight all the time. And I have to take medicine every day.

Righting a wrong

Justice *can* mean 'making amends when something bad happens'.

To get justice, Imelda could take the company who runs the factory to court.

It would feel fair if a court acknowledged that the company has done something wrong.

And the company should give Melia compensation, to pay for her medical bills. It's only fair!

Are the rules fair?

Justice is *also* 'a fair set of rules about what's right and wrong'.

In this case, Melia will only get compensation if there are fair rules that protect her from pollution.

Do the people who write our laws think it is OK for a factory to make people ill?

Fair treatment

Justice also means 'everyone being treated equally before the law'.

Melia must be treated fairly within the legal system. She must have the same chance as anyone else of getting compensation.

"Will a judge take her seriously?"

"How will Imelda afford a lawyer?"

"I bet the factory owners can afford a top lawyer."

Fair odds?

Another element of justice is whether some people in society are more likely than others to end up in a horrible situation like Melia's in the first place.

"Pollution is often really bad in poor neighbourhoods like ours. It's not fair. Something has to change. Our kids deserve to breathe clean air."

Justice across a whole society is known as **social justice**. In what we call a 'just' society, everyone has the same chances in life. But sadly, people facing hurdles such as poverty, racism, or both, are more likely to have a hard time getting basic things – from good education, to safe homes, to justice within the legal system.

Are laws just?

Most people agree that the purpose of laws is to deliver justice – but that doesn't mean they always do. Sometimes laws create *injustice too*.

Different treatment

Some laws make life harder for certain people. This kind of direct discrimination written into law is getting less common around the world. But in recent history, there are plenty of examples of laws that discriminate, or allow discrimination.

Until 2018, women weren't allowed to drive in Saudi Arabia.

Until 1970 in the United Kingdom, men could legally be paid more than women for doing exactly the same job.

In the 1930s, Hitler brought in laws that banned Jewish people in Germany from owning property, or running their own businesses.

Until 1965, poor Black people in the United States weren't allowed to vote.

Until 2021, transgender people were not allowed to serve in the US military.

A new law in India in 2019 gave many migrants the right to become citizens, but excluded Muslims.

Same-sex relationships are still punishable by the death sentence in more than 10 countries.

Different burden

Some laws apply to everyone, even though people aren't all in the same situation. For example, in many countries, a law says that people must pay money to the government – tax – every time they buy certain products.

I've just bought this tent and I have to pay £20 in tax on the purchase.

Same here! Can't wait to go camping.

I don't think the way that tax works is fair.

I didn't even think about the tax. It's the same law for everyone, so it's fair, right?

But paying an extra £20 matters more to me, because I have less money to spend.

Oh. OK. Well, if you're so poor, why buy the tent at all?

Because everyone deserves some enjoyment, however little money you have.

Well yes, when you put it like that, I see what you mean.

Falling short

Some people feel that there are important laws *missing*, which could help tackle injustice.

We need new laws giving everyone the same education. If rich kids keep getting a better one, the gap between rich and poor families stays really big.

I want an international law forcing countries causing the climate crisis to pay money to poor countries which suffer the most terrible impacts.

I want a new law saying that the US government must pay compensation to Black people whose ancestors were enslaved. Slavery has left many Black families at a disadvantage for generations.

Laws just like these could be created, especially if enough people supported them. It's important to keep debating what would make the world a more just place, and which laws might help it get there.

...more likely to have access to a competent lawyer?

Read more on p96-97.

...more likely to get a favourable decision from a judge?

I knew I could rely on Judge Newlyn. She's friends with my Uncle.

...more likely to have a judge or jury rule against them, because of prejudice or stereotypes?

The jury didn't believe me that my boyfriend attacked me.

Maybe they had it in their heads that women are only ever hurt by strangers.

But that's not true.

I know it isn't. But lots of people believe it.

...more likely to be able to launch a civil case?

Someone wrote a blog full of lies about me.

That happened to me too!

It's called libel. I took the person to court and I was awarded $50,000 in damages.

Oh wow! I didn't know you could do that.

My Dad's a lawyer so he explained what to do. You have to take action quite soon after the lies are published.

I wish I'd had some help. It's probably too late for me to do anything now.

If the legal system where you live does treat some people differently, find out what to do about it on page 87 and on pages 116-117.

Although every legal case *should* be fair, any system will go wrong *sometimes*. It's the job of appeal courts to put right any mistakes (see p28-29). But a legal system *shouldn't* be more likely to fail for some people than others.

95

The price of justice

Law is complicated and most people need lawyers to help make sense of it all. But hiring a lawyer is very expensive. To make matters worse, sometimes the people who need a lawyer most are those that can least afford it.

"My landlord wants to throw me out of my home, so he's changed the locks. I've lived there for 10 years and I've done nothing wrong."

A lawyer could persuade a court that this man should be allowed to stay in his home.

"I have a learning disability and I need help with everyday tasks. But the government has rejected my application for money to help me live independently."

A lawyer could persuade a court that the government should pay Sasha financial support, called **welfare** or **benefits**.

"I'm Ilhan. I've been sacked from my job. I think it was because they didn't like me being a Muslim."

A lawyer could help prove that Ilhan's employer discriminated against her so should pay her compensation.

"I've been accused of a crime that I didn't do."

A lawyer could defend him in court and help prove his innocence.

"I'm a lawyer. I charge *this* much for one hour of my time."

"I can't afford that. I'm a cleaner in a hospital and I don't even earn that much in a week."

"Me neither. I need every penny I have for rent, bills and food."

"Same here."

"Me too. So what can we do about it?"

Legal aid

To help poorer people get a fair outcome in court, some lawyers work for free, called **pro bono**, or only charge for their time *if* their client wins their case. In many places, the government pays for legal support too, called **legal aid**.

This *sounds* good. But a person relying on legal aid is often still at a disadvantage compared to someone who can afford to pay for a lawyer with their own money.

Does this mean that poorer people are always going to be less likely to get justice? What do you think?

Law enforcement

The job of the police is to enforce the law. But every year in the United States, hundreds of people are killed by the police. What's worse is that Black people are *three times more likely* to be killed by the police than White people. Why on earth is this? And what can be done?

How come police are killing people? Aren't you supposed to be protecting us?

Well sometimes in our job we need to use deadly force – that's enough force that it kills someone – to protect ourselves, or someone else.

So you're saying that you're allowed to kill someone if that person is behaving very dangerously?

Well actually, the law says we can use deadly force if we think someone is *about* to get dangerous.

If you *think?!?* How long do you spend thinking about it before you decide what to do?

We have to make very quick decisions. Sometimes there are just seconds between assessing a situation and firing a gun.

It's terrifying that you are making split-second judgments about people! I'm scared that, because of racism, some police officers are more likely to assume a Black person is dangerous!

You are right. Racism is all around us, and inside everyone. And it gets expressed, especially in moments of extreme tension.

A police officer could see danger when it isn't there. They might assume someone is reaching for a weapon, when they are just reaching for their phone.

I'm afraid that does happen sometimes.

This makes me so upset and angry.

This is not just a problem in the US. In many other countries, police officers are also much more likely to use deadly force against Black people. And it's rare for a police officer who kills someone to be convicted of a crime.

Fighting for justice

Many people are outraged about this and big protests take place frequently in the US, and beyond. Protesters call for justice, but what exactly do they mean?

PROTECT BLACK LIVES

Justice means valuing Black lives as much as White lives.

PUNISH VIOLENT POLICE

Justice means remembering and honouring the people who died.

JUSTICE FOR

Sandra Bland
George Floyd
Laquan McDonald
Michael Brown
Eric Garner
Philando Castile
Breonna Taylor
Tamir Rice
Alton Sterling
Freddie Gray
Walter Scott
Jamar Clark
Stephon Clark

Justice means punishing the police officers who use excessive, unnecessary force against Black people. It's horrific that they get away with it so often.

I think that justice means changing the law. How can it be legal to use deadly force SO often?

If the police officers were punished every time, it would put other people officers off using violence.

END POLICE VIOLENCE

BLACK LIVES MATTER

To me, justice means making sure this STOPS HAPPENING. We need to challenge racism in all its forms.

Justice means changing the way governments spend money serving Black communities. I think we need FAR fewer police officers, and more money spent on healthcare and housing.

Who has the power?

Judges have lots of power. But in many places, judges don't properly reflect the **diversity** of society – meaning differences in race, gender, religion, sexuality, disability or family wealth. But why does diversity matter?

I would much prefer to have a judge who was similar to me. Otherwise I worry he or she might be prejudiced against me. I might be found guilty, even if I'm not!

It's the job of judges to be impartial, and they are guided by written laws, so does it really make a difference?

But there are grey areas in law, and in these bits, judges' decisions are surely influenced by their own life experiences.

But if a judge is surrounded by a diverse group of other judges, at least they can consult each other on different perspectives.

But that's the problem! There are *hardly any* judges who look and sound like me. It makes me feel like the system isn't there to serve *me* at all.

Oh no! It's not good for society for people to feel like that.

I know. I see law a bit like a contract. People generally obey laws, and in return, the legal system deals with any problems.

But if the system doesn't work for us, why do we bother obeying laws?

Well, I wonder that, sometimes.

The most powerful judges are those at the highest courts, where decisions are typically made on the most complicated or important cases. But there is the least diversity at the highest level. For example, in 2020, all these things were true.

A **Black woman** had never been a Supreme Court judge in the United States.

All around the world, you were more likely to become a senior judge if you were from **a rich family**.

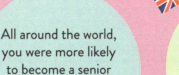

There had never been any judge – male or female – who wasn't **White** on the UK's Supreme Court.

Only 10% of senior judges in India were **women**.

Hardly anywhere had an equal split of men and women. But it is possible – in Zambia, more than half of senior judges were **women**.

There had never been an **Indigenous*** judge on the highest court of Canada or Australia.

* 'Indigenous' means someone whose family lived in those places long before European settlers arrived there. (See page 39)

Becoming a judge

The route to becoming a judge varies in different places. In some, you work as a lawyer first for many years. In others, you can train as a judge directly. Law firms or governments can increase diversity by running schemes to encourage young people from a range of backgrounds to train in the law.

This is Grace Helen Whitener, a senior judge in the state of Washington in the United States.

This is Rabinder Singh, a senior judge in England.

I'm a lesbian, female, Black, disabled, immigrant judge.

It's crucial to support and mentor young people from backgrounds that aren't yet represented in the legal profession.

The more that people see a diverse group of judges, the more people from every social background will feel they can be judges too.

Why are some people violent?

Is it more important to keep people safe, or give them privacy?

Do lawyers ever defend people they KNOW are guilty?

7. Big questions

Even though our legal systems have been around for centuries, there are still some big questions that don't have clear answers.

This chapter explores some things you might be wondering, such as "Does prison work?" – as well as others you might not have thought of yet, such as "Can rivers have rights?"

Not everyone agrees how best to use law to look after people and the environment. Read some of the different arguments and make up your own mind.

Does prison work?

Although criminals are held in prisons all around the world, not everyone agrees about whether prisons actually *work*.

Prison is supposed to be a way to keep everyone in society safe. *But does it?*

Prison is supposed to be a fair punishment for the crime that someone commits. *But is it?*

> Prisons keep people safe! They take very dangerous people out of society and stop them from causing harm.

> I was attacked. Then for months I was too scared to go outside. I lost *my* freedom, so it feels fair that the man who did it also lost *his* freedom for a while.

> But prisons themselves can be dangerous for prisoners and staff.

> That's especially true when they are overcrowded, without enough prison guards.

> I went to prison. But I think I have been punished twice. Once doing the time behind bars....

> ...and now also because, having been to prison, no one will give me a job.

> I think I was punished as well and I didn't hurt anyone. I hardly got to see my Dad while he was locked up. That's not fair!

> OK so maybe prisons only keep some people safe?

Prison is supposed to put people off committing crime. *But does it?*

"No! I broke the law because I was desperate. I didn't even think about the threat of going to prison."

"I'm not scared of prison, as I don't think I'll get caught. If the police were better at catching criminals, maybe I would be put off."

Prison is supposed to help criminals turn away from crime. *Does it?*

"Yes! Prison gave me a wake-up call to change my life and move away from crime."

"Yes! I was in a violent situation at home. Going to prison gave me a chance to get help and change my life."

"Yes! I learned to read while I was behind bars. I had a teacher who helped me see the point of it."

"No! I was a teenager when I went to prison, for a minor crime. Inside, I learned how to commit much more serious crimes!"

"No! I started taking drugs for the first time inside prison. It created many more problems for me."

"No! I wasn't given the chance to do anything meaningful inside prison."

On average, around half of people released from prison go on to commit another crime. This happens much less if prisons offer training and other support for inmates. But if a prisoner isn't dangerous, is it better to offer this to criminals outside of a prison (see alternative sentences on page 26)? What do you think?

Why are some people violent?

When one person hurts another, there's a strong instinct to want justice: to catch them and punish them. But *why* are some people violent? And how can violent crime be prevented in the first place?

Violent criminals are sometimes assumed just to be "bad people", who choose to hurt someone. But researchers find that people are *more likely* to be violent if they have a hard time when they are growing up. Here are a few examples.

Violent family

Children who see violence at home are more likely to grow up to be violent themselves, because they learn that behaviour.

No opportunities

Having few options in life can make people feel rejected and angry, which can lead to violence. This can be because they have never been taught to read, or live in a run-down neighbourhood with no jobs.

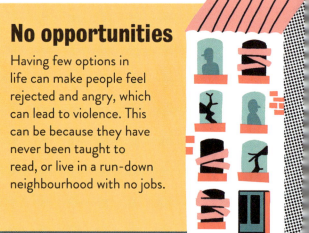

Uncaring carers

When parents or caregivers are unreliable and unemotional, children struggle to learn how to have healthy relationships. Children looked after by the authorities, rather than their family, are at particular risk.

Addiction

Using drugs or alcohol makes someone more likely to be violent. Someone vulnerable, for example a young person without a loving family, is more likely to get addicted to drugs or alcohol.

These are known as **risk factors** for violence. Someone who experiences these things may find it *harder* to choose to avoid violence.

How come some people have these experiences but *still* avoid violence? Researchers think it may be due to some positive things in their life, such as:

- A positive adult role model – someone to look up to and admire
- Good skills at resolving conflicts
- Feeling proud of achievements at school

In Scotland, violent crime has fallen dramatically since the year 2009. This is thanks to schemes supporting people at risk of committing violence.

Here are some examples.

Support workers visit people in hospital who've been injured in a fight.

"Can I help you with anything? Here's my number. Call me if you want to talk."

"Nobody ever asked me that before. Maybe they can help me quit drinking alcohol?"

Schools in rough neighbourhoods help children manage their emotions and resolve conflicts.

"A girl laughed at my shirt."

"How did that make you feel?"

"A bit sad."

A café in Glasgow gives jobs to people who have been convicted for violent crime.

"My job gives me the structure and skills I need to get my life back on track."

"I have a **mentor** at the café, who looks out for me. She's a great role model."

This way of reducing violence is called a **public health** approach. That's because it treats violence like an illness spreading between people, not simply a choice to commit an evil act. With this approach, people outside the justice system help solve a problem to do with justice – it's not just about police, lawyers and judges.

Defending the guilty

Do lawyers ever stand up in court and defend someone that they know is guilty? Is that allowed? Just like many things in law, the answer is a little complex.

For example, imagine this situation.

What happens above is NOT allowed. A lawyer can't lie to a court or allow a witness to give false evidence. However, a lawyer rarely knows *for sure* if their client is guilty...

This second version of events IS allowed, and is much more common.

A lawyer focuses on whether the prosecution's evidence is strong enough for a jury to convict their client – in other words whether they are "legally guilty", rather than if they *actually* committed the crime, known as "factually guilty".

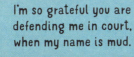

Can tech help solve crimes?

When it's linked up to a camera or sensor, a computer can sort through information and spot patterns quickly. This makes it a powerful tool for police and security agencies. Here's some of the technology on offer.

Special facial recognition cameras scan passersby to see if their faces match those of people on police watch lists.

Planes equipped with a special device can search for a suspect by tracking their mobile phone signal.

As the plane flies over, every mobile phone in the area connects to the device. A computer then picks out the wanted mobile's signal and locates the phone.

Speed cameras photograph speeding cars. A computer then matches the car's number plate to a registered address and sends a fine.

Security agencies can also use computers to sift through people's online activity to spot if there's anything dodgy going on.

Swimming pool opening times

Who would win in a fight? Batman or Spider-Man?

How do you make a bomb?

What's the catch?

These kinds of technology are designed to make people feel safer. But as technology gets more powerful it threatens people's right to **privacy**. Should *everyone* be watched, just to catch the *few* that break the law?

I help keep you SAFE. Police officers can't be everywhere all the time, so having extra pairs of eyes helps them to do their job.

But you're recording information about everyone, even if they haven't done anything wrong. You're treating us *all* like CRIMINALS!

If you've got nothing to hide what's the problem?

I have a right not to be watched unless you have a good reason to think I've done something *wrong*. What if you see me doing something embarrassing?

Don't worry, if you're innocent we'll delete the footage.

But can I trust you? Who monitors the information that you're collecting? What if you sell it to companies?

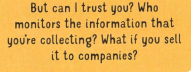

Well, you trust your phone, which scans your face and knows where you are. So what's the difference?

Well, maybe I shouldn't trust EITHER of you!

It's a tricky debate — for lawmakers and courts too. How do you protect people's privacy? What information should security agencies be allowed to collect? Courts in the US and Europe have tended to judge that targeting suspects is *ok*, but spying on everyone *isn't*. For example, a security agency could look through a suspect's phone records, but it wouldn't be allowed to monitor everyone's phones.

Can rivers have rights?

What if the natural world, from trees, to rivers, to animals, had rights – just like people? In 2008, Ecuador became the first country in the world to recognize rights for nature in its constitution. This means that if someone harms nature, in the eyes of the law it's as if they are hurting a person.

In 2011, some local government builders dumped rubbish in the Vilcabamba river. So the representatives for the river took the builders to court.

Dumping rubbish causes the river to flood and harms the people who live by it!

Ouch!

The court ruled in favour of the river. It made the government clean up and apologize.

Giving nature legal rights is also a way of respecting the rights of the people who have a deep connection with the land. After a 140-year legal battle, in 2017 a Maori tribe in New Zealand succeeded in having the Whanganui river recognized as a legal person.

We consider the river to be an ancestor of our tribe. We've lived and depended on it for over 700 years.

What if animals owned their homes?

Tens of thousands of animal species die out, or become **extinct**, every year. One of the biggest threats they face is the destruction of their homes because of pollution, cutting down trees or building.

In many countries there are already *some* laws that protect animal homes.

It's usually illegal to disturb or take a nest even if it's on 'your' land.

The idea of giving some animals *ownership* goes one step further than protection. Legally, it would work as a **trust** – which is when a person holds property for the benefit of someone else. In this set-up, some land would belong to animals but be managed *by* humans *for* the animals.

Which animals?

Animals come and go, so rather than specific species owning land, it would be owned by the **ecosystem** – the community of living things in the area.

Which humans?

Only wildlife experts would be allowed to manage the trust and they'd have to follow strict rules.

I'm off, but my family will be back next year!

Mmmm, I'm not sure I trust any humans to manage the land on our behalf.

No idea is perfect, nor will it solve the *whole* problem.
But people would have to take into account the interests of animals on animal-owned land, in a way that they don't when it's owned by humans.

Could I be a lawyer?

How do I get better at arguing?

Do lawyers make good presidents?

8. What next?

Law isn't simple, is it? Setting clear, fair rules that people will actually follow can sometimes seem impossible. But do you know what? All the knotty issues are what makes law so interesting.

If you agree, read on to find out what YOU can do to explore the world of law, including how to create or change laws yourself, and how to decide if you want to have a job in law one day.

Get stuck in

There are all sorts of practical things that you can do to find out more about law, and learn useful skills along the way.

Watch a trial

Many trials are open to the public. You can find out what's on by telephoning your local court, or looking at its website.

See inside policing

In some places, it's possible to become a police cadet. Police cadets go on activity camps, learn first aid skills, help out at community events and even support police investigations.

Help make the rules

Some schools have a **school council**. This is a group of students who are elected to represent their classmates. School councils are a way for students to have their say in issues that affect them at school.

"Please can the timetable be adjusted? There isn't enough time between our lessons."

"We always have to rush from one to the next, which means we end up getting told off for running in the halls."

"What an interesting proposal. Thank you for raising this."

If there isn't one at your school yet, you could propose one. If you don't want to be on the school council yourself, you could help a friend who you think would do a good job to get elected.

Change the law

Organizing activities to try to change a law is known as **campaigning**. Look out for a campaign that you care about. This might be to stop an unpopular law coming in, to introduce a new law that doesn't exist yet, or to get a current law applied more fairly between people.

You could:
- Go on a protest.
- Share messages from charities or other campaigning organizations.
- Write to your political representative.

Learn to debate

A **debate** is a structured argument about a specific topic. Two teams take opposite sides of the argument. They each have the same amount of time to speak and try to make their side seem the most convincing. Debating helps you...

- ...look at an issue from different angles.
- ...form opinions about issues.
- ...build your research skills.
- ...speak in front of people.
- ...explain why you think something.

These are exactly the skills that lawyers, politicians and campaigners need. Some schools have debating clubs. If your school doesn't, you could start one.

Hold a mock trial

A mock trial is another activity for a class or youth club. You could set one up about a historical figure, a fictional character, or even an animal. Everyone in the group is allocated a role: the accused, lawyers, witnesses, a judge or the jury.

Bats, you stand accused of spreading the virus Covid-19 to humans.

We plead not guilty!

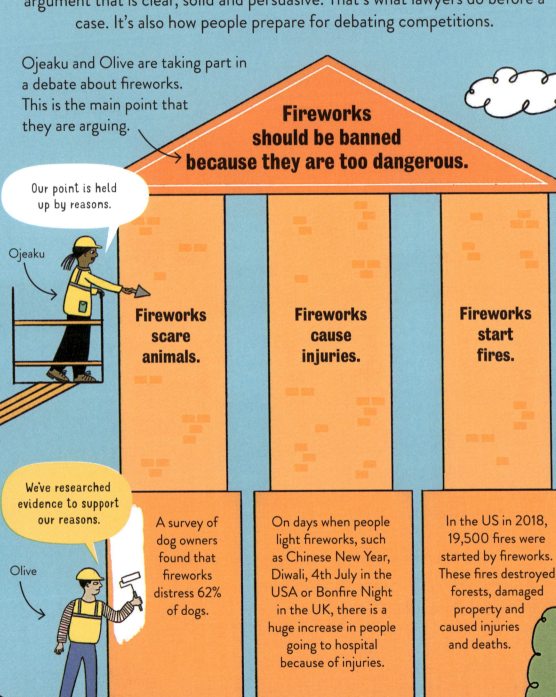

As well as preparing their own argument, Olive and Ojeaku try to guess the argument that their opponents in the competition might be building.

"Let's find the strongest argument AGAINST what we are saying?"

www.fireworks.com — If fireworks were illegal, then people would make and sell them secretly. Fireworks might be even more dangerous, because they wouldn't be controlled.

"Hmmm - how can we rebut that? Maybe we can say the police could just follow the flashes and bangs to catch people."

When it comes to the debate, Olive and Ojeaku each make a speech to present their argument. They speak clearly and choose their words carefully.

Ojeaku states her main point at the beginning, then explains the structure of their argument.

Using emotional language helps to get their audience on side.

Olive builds the counter argument and her rebuttal into her speech.

"There are three compelling reasons why fireworks should be banned, all backed up by solid evidence. Number one..."

"Is it fair for innocent animals to be left confused and terrified simply for the entertainment of human beings?"

"One might say that banning fireworks could lead to an uncontrolled market of illegal fireworks. Well, I say that..."

The most convincing arguments are well reasoned and backed by facts. This takes lots of planning (which is why lawyers sometimes stay up late the night before they go to court). But even the strongest arguments may not win the day, if people have made up their minds already.

"Great job, Ojeaku and Olive, but I still disagree with you. Fireworks are just too much fun to be banned."

CLAP CLAP

Jobs in law

If you're enjoying this book, perhaps you'd like a job related to law. Lots of jobs in law involve listening, talking and helping people. But which one might suit you best? Ask yourself these questions to find out.

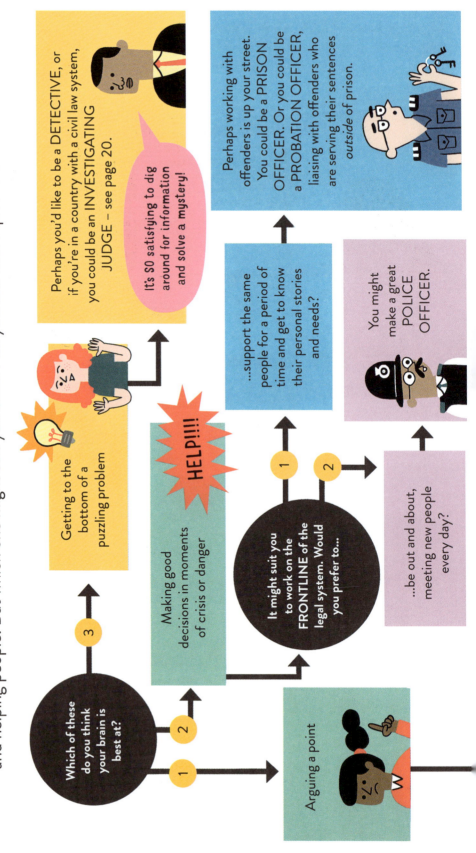

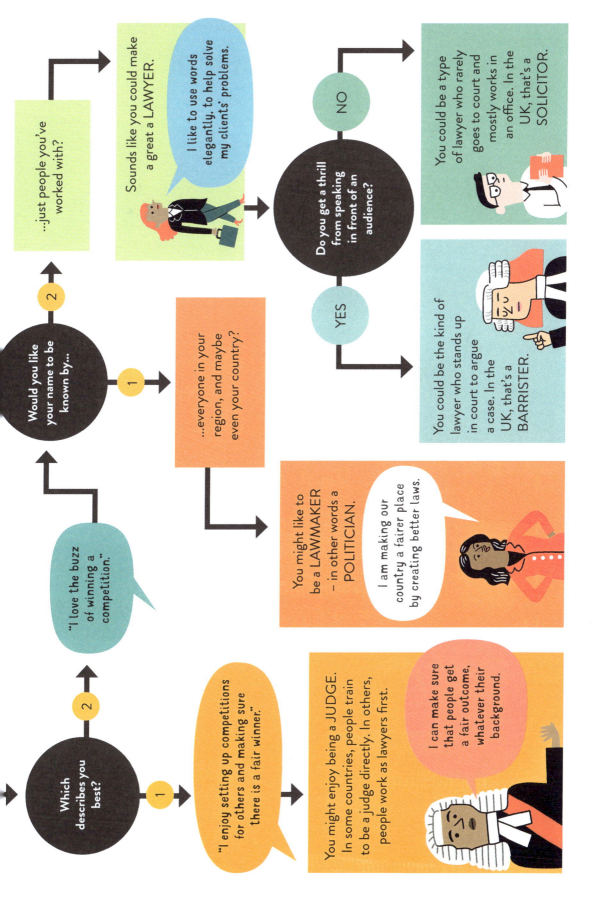

Have you heard of...

...Mandela, Gandhi and Veil? These inspirational figures from the last 150 years all trained as lawyers and used their knowledge of law to bring about great change.

Gandhi inspired millions to resist British occupation in India with non-violent protest.

Overcame his fear of public speaking while working as lawyer in South Africa

I resisted the British by breaking their laws and by peacefully submitting to arrest and imprisonment.

Was imprisoned many times for his activities

Mohandas Gandhi
Leader of the struggle for Indian independence from British rule
(Born in 1869, died in 1948)

I worked to get many women's rights protected by law, such as access to contraception for all women.

Received the Nobel Peace Prize for bringing a peaceful end to the Cold War between the Soviet Union, the US and their allies in 1990

Mikhail Gorbachev
Russian president
(Born 1931)

Simone Veil
French lawyer and lawmaker
(1927-2017)

All my life, I've defended victims of human rights abuses.

Worked as a lawyer before becoming a politician

As president, I successfully passed laws on affordable healthcare and legalized same-sex marriage.

Shirin Ebadi
Human rights lawyer and first female judge in Iran
(Born 1947)

Barack Obama
First Black president of the US
(Born 1961)

"As Minister for Justice, I created the Marriage Law in 1950, which made forced marriage illegal and improved women's rights."

Ran her own law firm in the 1930s in Shanghai

"Do you remember me? I was the lead lawyer in the Brown case on page 55, which led to the end of separate schools for Black and White children."

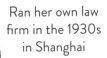

Shi Liang
Chinese lawyer and Minister for Justice
(1900-1985)

Thurgood Marshall
American civil rights lawyer and first Black Supreme Court Justice
(1908-1993)

Nelson Mandela led the fight against the way South Africa was run, known as **apartheid**. Apartheid divided people by race and denied Black people many rights

Started the first Black-owned law firm in South Africa

"I spent 27 years in prison for trying to end apartheid. When I was released in 1990, I led the efforts to end White rule and to rebuild the country peacefully."

Awarded the Nobel Peace Prize in 1993

Nelson Mandela
Revolutionary leader and first Black president of South Africa
(1918-2013)

There are so many lawyers working today to make the world a better place. Who knows, one day your name could be added to this list...

Yetnebersh Nigussie set up the Ethiopian Centre for disability and development.

Lewis Pugh is a maritime lawyer who helped to create the largest protected area in the world in the Antarctic Ocean.

Ana María Arboleda Perdomo is director of *Fundación ProBono Colombia*, which provides legal aid to people who can't afford legal services.

Why law matters

By now you'll know that the law isn't distant or remote – it touches us all. The law sets out what people *can* and *can't* do, and what happens when things go wrong. So it's really important to know about law and understand it, in order to make sure it's working for *everyone*.

Glossary

This glossary explains some of the words used in this book. Words written in *italic* type are explained in other entries.

accused, the a person who has been charged with committing a crime, but has not yet been found guilty.

appeal when a decision by a lower *court* is reconsidered by a higher *court*.

civil law laws to do with relationships between people, companies and organizations.

common law a system of law based on the decisions made by *judges* at previous *trials*.

compensation money paid to a victim to make up for being hurt.

constitution a set of fundamental rules and laws about how an organization or country is run.

contract an agreement between people to do, or not do, certain things.

court a place, or group of people, who have the power to hold *trials*.

criminal law laws to do with people causing harm to each other.

discrimination unfair treatment of a person because of something to do with the way they are, for example their gender or age.

evidence anything that helps to prove or disprove something in a *trial*.

hearing a session similar to a *trial*, but typically shorter and less formal.

human rights things every person should have, such as food and shelter.

judge a person who has the power to run a *court*, and to make decisions about the law.

jury a group of people, randomly chosen, who get to decide a *verdict* at some *trials*.

legal aid when the government gives people money to help them pay their legal costs.

penalty a punishment, such as paying a fine, given to a person who has done something wrong.

plea part of a *trial* when the *accused* declares that they are "guilty" or "not guilty" of a crime.

prosecute to use the law to bring someone accused of a crime to *trial*.

sue to accuse a person or institution of something according to *civil laws*.

Supreme Court in many countries, the most powerful group of *judges*.

treaty an agreement made between governments or countries.

trial when people meet to argue about a case, usually decided by a *judge* or *jury* in *court*.

verdict the final decision made at a *trial*, usually given by a *judge* or *jury*.

witness a person called to answer questions during a *trial*.

Index

amendments, 51, 54, 55
ancient Egypt, 8
ancient Rome, 8-9
animal rights, 79, 112, 113
appeals, 28-29, 33, 48, 95, 125
arbitration, 69
Australia, 39, 47, 101

bail, 19
barristers, 20, 22-23
Brown, Linda, 55, 123

civil law, 31-41, 95
civil law systems, 44, 46-47
colonization, 39, 67
common law, 44, 46-47, 48-49, 125
community service, 26-27
compensation, 26-27, 32, 33, 34, 35, 90-91, 93, 96, 125
constitutional law, 43-59
constitutions, 43, 52-57, 59, 112, 125
contracts, 7, 34-35, 62, 125
copyright, 40, 128
courts, 8, 19, 22-23, 28-29, 65, 116
Covid-19, 72-73
crimes, 15-29, 72, 73, 104-105
crimes against humanity, 65
criminal law, 15-29, 32, 47, 72-73, 125
customary laws, 45, 46, 47
customs, 11, 45, 56, 63

death sentences, 26, 92
debating, 117, 118-119
defamation, 32, 81
disability, 82, 84-85, 96, 100, 123
discrimination, 79, 82-83, 84-85, 86-87, 92, 125

diversity, 100-101
divorce, 36, 82

England, 15, 18, 20, 22, 48, 53, 57, 94
environment, 103, 112-113
Europe, 20, 47, 57, 73
evidence, 9, 16-25, 28, 29, 55, 108-109, 125
extraditions, 73

fair trial, 22, 73, 78, 109
family law, 36-37
fines, 5, 6, 9, 26, 125
France, 46, 47, 50-51, 64
fraud, 32
freedom of expression, 80-81

Geneva convention, 71
Germany, 47, 58-59, 72, 92
guilt, 8, 9, 12, 19, 22-25, 29, 108-109

hate speech, 81
Hitler, Adolf, 59, 92
hostage crisis, 68-69
human rights, 63, 70, 77-87, 125
  abuses, 81, 122

India, 47, 92, 101, 122
intellectual property, 40
international courts, 62, 65, 68, 82
international law, 61-75, 93
Interpol, 72, 73
intersectionality, 83
Iran, 68, 69, 122
Islamic law, 45, 46, 47

jobs in law, 120-121
judge-made laws, 48-49

126

Acknowledgments

Written by
Rose Hall and Lara Bryan

Illustrated by
Miguel Bustos and Anna Wray

Edited by
Alex Frith

Designed by
Freya Harrison

Series editor:
Jane Chisholm

Series designer:
Stephen Moncrieff

Expert advice from barristers Natasha Jackson and Will Martin; and from Show Racism the Red Card

Additional illustration by Ian McNee

With thanks to Peri Cheal, Beth Cox and Emily Frith

First published in 2021 by Usborne Publishing Ltd., Usborne House, 83-85 Saffron Hill, London, EC1N 8RT, United Kingdom. usborne.com

This bit is a legal way to stop people from copying the words and pictures in this book and passing them off as their own work.

Copyright © 2021 Usborne Publishing Ltd. The name Usborne and the Balloon logo are Trade Marks of Usborne Publishing Ltd. All rights reserved. No part of this publication may be reproduced, stored in any retrieval system, or transmitted in any form or by any means without the prior permission of the publisher. UKE.

The websites recommended at Usborne Quicklinks are regularly reviewed but Usborne Publishing is not responsible and does not accept liability for the availability or content of any website other than its own, or for any exposure to harmful, offensive or inaccurate material which may appear on the Web. Usborne Publishing will have no liability for any damage or loss caused by viruses that may be downloaded as a result of browsing the sites it recommends.

judges, 5, 9, 19, 20, 23, 25, 26, 29, 44,
    48-49, 58-59, 65, 100, 101, 121
juries, 19, 20, 22-25, 95, 109, 117, 125
justice, 9, 89-101, 106, 124

Lady Justice, 9
lawmakers, 77, 81, 111, 121, 122
lawyers, 8, 17, 18, 20, 22, 23, 96, 97,
    108-109, 121,
    famous, 123
legal aid, 97, 123, 124
legal codes, 44, 47
legal systems, 44-47, 91, 94, 95, 103
legislative branch, 44, 58, 59
libel, 95

Mandela, Nelson, 40, 122, 123
marriage, 11, 36-37, 92, 122, 123
Marshall, Thurgood, 123
mediation, 41, 69
medical law, 49
morals, 10-11, 90
murder, 8, 10, 17, 18, 20, 26, 29, 48,
    59, 65

negligence, 33
New Zealand, 47, 80, 112

parliaments, 5, 43, 44, 46, 47, 50-51,
    56, 57, 59
patents, 40
police, 5, 13, 15-19, 72, 73, 86, 94, 98,
    99, 107, 110, 111, 116, 117, 121
pollution, 35, 62, 65, 82, 90, 91, 113
prisons, 5, 26, 79, 81, 103, 104-105
privacy, 111
pro bono, 97
property law, 38-39
prosecutors, 18
protests, 7, 40, 68, 84-85, 99, 117, 123

racism, 55, 91, 98, 99
rehabilitation, 26
religious law, 45, 46, 47
rights, 7, 36, 37, 54, 55, 59, 63, 64, 66,
    70, 77-87, 103, 123, 125
rule of law, 59

sanctions, 64
Scotland, 33, 46, 57, 107
seas, 74-75
self-defence, 64, 70
separation of powers, 58-59
slavery, 54, 65, 93
snails, 33
solicitors, 20
South Africa, 46, 122, 123
space, 74
statutes, 44
supreme courts, 39, 44, 53, 55, 56, 101,
    123, 125

technology, 110-111
theft, 12-13, 125
torts, 32
treaties, 59, 62-63, 64, 74, 75, 125
trials, 19, 22-23, 48, 116, 117, 125
trusts, 113

UK, 53, 56, 57, 64, 84, 92, 97, 101
United Nations (UN), 63, 64-65, 66,
    67, 70, 78
USA, 44, 46, 53, 54, 55, 64, 68, 69,
    92, 93, 98, 99, 101, 111, 122

verdicts, 19, 24-25, 28, 125
violence, 106-107

wars, 60, 63, 70-71
wigs, 23
witnesses, 20, 22, 108, 125